Avoidant Attachment Detox

Embrace Emotional Intimacy, Recognize Dismissive Patterns, and Uncover Deactivation Triggers to Nurture Lasting Relationships - Daily Exercises for Secure Connection

A.J BROOKS

Copyright © 2024 by A.J BROOKS

All rights reserved.

No portion of this book may be reproduced in any form without written permission from the publisher or author, except as permitted by U.S. copyright law.This publication is designed to provide accurate and authoritative information in regard to the subject matter covered.

It is sold with the understanding that neither the author nor the publisher is engaged in rendering legal, investment, accounting or other professional services.

While the publisher and author have used their best efforts in preparing this book, they make no representations or warranties with respect to the accuracy or completeness of the contents of this book and specifically disclaim any implied warranties of merchantability or fitness for a particular purpose.

No warranty may be created or extended by sales representatives or written sales materials. The advice and strategies contained herein may not be suitable for your situation.

You should consult with a professional when appropriate. Neither the publisher nor the author shall be liable for any loss of profit or any other commercial damages, including but not limited to special, incidental, consequential, personal, or other damages.

Contents

Introduction	vii
1. FOUNDATIONS OF AVOIDANT ATTACHMENT	1
The Psychology Behind Avoidant Attachment	1
Identifying Dismissive-Avoidant Behaviors in Daily Life	3
The Impact of Childhood Experiences on Attachment Style	5
A Brain's Perspective on Emotional Detachment	7
Misconceptions About Avoidant Attachment Debunked	9
2. RECOGNIZING AVOIDANT TENDENCIES	13
The Spectrum of Avoidance: From Mild to Severe	13
Self-Assessment: Are You Subconsciously Avoiding Intimacy?	15
Deactivation Strategies: How You Unknowingly Sabotage Connections	17
Emotional Numbing: Signs and Solutions	19
The Avoidant's Inner Dialogue: Understanding Your Thought Patterns	21
3. THE ANATOMY OF AVOIDANT RELATIONSHIPS	25
Romantic Pitfalls: Navigating Love as an Avoidant	
The Avoidant in Friendships: Balancing Independence and Closeness	
Family Dynamics: The Role of Avoidant Attachment	
The Anxious-Avoidant Trap: Understanding the Push and Pull	
Professional Relationships: Achieving Connection Without Vulnerability	
Solitude vs. Loneliness: Reconciling the Need for Space	

4. THE POWER OF SELF-AWARENESS 39
   Mindfulness Practices to Observe Avoidant Behaviors 39
   Identifying Your Triggers: What Pushes You Away? 41
   The Power of Pause: Reflecting Before Retreating 43
   Emotional Literacy: Naming and Understanding Your Feelings 45

5. EMBRACING VULNERABILITY FOR STRONGER BONDS 49
   Small Steps Towards Trust: Gradual Exposure to Vulnerability 49
   Revisiting Past Hurts: Healing Old Wounds 51
   Vulnerability in Action: Practical Exercises for Everyday Life 54
   Setting Boundaries: Vulnerability Without Overexposure 57
   The Role of Self-Compassion in Embracing Vulnerability 59

6. SHADOW WORK AND INNER HEALING 63
   Introduction to Shadow Work for Avoidants 63
   Unearthing Hidden Fears: The Shadow of Independence 65
   Re-parenting Yourself: Healing Childhood Wounds 67
   Integrating the Shadow for Wholeness and Connection 69

7. PRACTICAL STRATEGIES TO HEAL THE GAP 73
   Rewriting the Narrative: Positive Affirmations for the Avoidant 73
   The Role of Therapy: Finding the Right Help 76
   Communicating Needs: Scripts and Strategies 78
   Rebuilding Trust: Steps Toward Secure Attachment 80
   Self-Soothing Techniques for Anxiety and Fear 82
   Visualization for Emotional Healing and Connection 84
   The Art of Apology: Repairing After Retreat 87

8. EXERCISES FOR COUPLES TO MOVE INTO SECURE
   ATTACHMENT   91
   Dialogue Exercises to Enhance Connection   91
   Building Empathy: The Two-Sided Story
   Technique   93
   Partner Exercises for Continuous Emotional
   Growth   95
   The Appreciation List: Fostering Gratitude in
   Relationships   97
   Conflict Resolution Skills for a Stronger Bond   99
   Planning Future Dreams Together to Strengthen
   Bonds   102

9. DEEPENING EMOTIONAL INTIMACY   105
   Emotional Availability: Becoming Present in Your
   Relationships   105
   Active Listening: Techniques for Empathetic
   Engagement   108
   Expressing Affection: Finding Your Love Language   109
   Receiving Love: Overcoming the Discomfort of
   Being Cared For   111
   The Importance of Physical Touch in Building
   Connection   113

10. NAVIGATING EMOTIONAL DETOX   117
    Emotional Detox: Letting Go of Suppressed
    Feelings   117
    Techniques for Safe Emotional Release   119
    The Role of Self-Compassion in Healing Avoidant
    Attachment   121
    Rebuilding Your Emotional Toolbox: Skills for
    Connection   124
    From Isolation to Integration: Steps Towards
    Emotional Openness   126

11. SUSTAINING GROWTH AND CONNECTION   129
    Maintaining Momentum: Strategies to Prevent
    Backsliding   129
    Celebrating Progress: Recognizing and Rewarding
    Change   131

Community and Support Systems: Finding Your Tribe	133
The Lifelong Journey: Embracing Growth Beyond Avoidance	136
Outro	139
References	143

Introduction

Have you ever found yourself pushing away someone you care about, not because you don't value them, but because closeness feels too risky, too vulnerable? Perhaps there's a voice inside you whispering for intimacy and connection, but another, louder voice warns you to retreat to safety. You're not alone in this struggle. Many, just like you, navigate these conflicting desires daily, often without understanding why or how to manage them.

This is where "Avoidant Attachment Detox" comes into play. This book aims to guide you, someone with a dismissive and avoidant attachment style, toward healing, deeper self-awareness, and enriched relationships. This transformation is not limited to your romantic endeavors; it also encompasses your friendships and family ties, weaving a broader fabric of emotional connectedness.

You might recognize the challenges: a lingering fear of intimacy, relationships that seem never to last, and a paradoxical longing for closeness that you feel compelled to suppress. These are common experiences for those with avoidant attachment, and they stem from deeper, often unexplored parts of your emotional landscape.

This book offers a unique approach by integrating attachment theory, practical exercises, and shadow work. It provides a clear, actionable path toward changing your relationship with intimacy. We'll explore these strategies not just in theory but as tools you can apply in your daily life to initiate real change.

My passion for helping individuals like you stems from a blend of professional dedication and personal experience. I believe deeply in the potential for transformation that lies within each of us. Through my work, I've seen firsthand the powerful shifts that can occur when individuals commit to exploring the depths of their attachment styles.

In the following pages, we will begin by understanding the roots of avoidant attachment, move through pathways to healing these old wounds, and finally, learn how to enhance and embrace emotional connections. Each section builds upon the last, facilitating a gradual and sustainable transformation, ensuring that you are always moving forward on your journey.

Embarking on this journey requires patience, self-compassion, and a commitment to delve into sometimes challenging emotional territories. Approach this book with an open mind, ready to engage with each exercise and reflection thoughtfully.

There is immense potential for growth and improved relationships ahead. Envision a future where you can engage in healthy, intimate relationships without fear. While the path may have its challenges, the rewards—deeper connections and a more fulfilling emotional life—are profound and within your grasp.

I invite you to join me on this transformative journey. Use this book as your roadmap to a richer, more connected life. The change won't happen overnight, but with each step, you'll be closer to a life where relationships are not sources of fear but foundations of strength.

Let's begin this journey together with the hope and belief that change is not only possible but within your reach. Together, we can work towards a future rich with meaningful, enduring connections.

Chapter 1
Foundations of Avoidant Attachment

When you receive a message from someone close, do you often find yourself hesitating to reply, not out of disinterest but from an inexplicable urge to maintain distance? This reaction, seemingly trivial on the surface, might be rooted in something much deeper and pervasive—your attachment style. For many, understanding why they react the way they do in relationships can be both a revelation and a first step toward meaningful change. This chapter delves into the psychology behind avoidant attachment, tracing its origins and the fundamental ways it shapes your interactions and internal life.

The Psychology Behind Avoidant Attachment

Avoidant attachment is commonly characterized by a strong desire for independence, often appearing at the expense of close relationships. This attachment style is not about cherishing solitude above all else; instead, it emerges from a deep-seated need to protect oneself from the perceived risks of intimacy. For you, like many others with this style, independence isn't just a preference. It's a necessity, a crucial defense mechanism against the vulnerability that comes with emotional dependence on others.

The concept of avoidant attachment finds its roots in the seminal work of John Bowlby and Mary Ainsworth, who introduced Attachment Theory in the mid-20th century. Bowlby posited that the bonds formed between children and their primary caregivers have profound impacts that extend well into adulthood. Ainsworth later identified three significant styles of attachment—secure, anxious, and avoidant—through her famous "Strange Situation" study, where children's reactions to separation from and reunion with their parents were observed. The children who seemed indifferent to these separations were classified as avoidant. They appeared self-sufficient, yet beneath that veneer of independence often lay a well of unmet needs and suppressed emotions.

Understanding avoidant attachment involves more than just psychological theories; it's also about the biology underpinning our behaviors. The brain's fear and reward systems play crucial roles in this attachment style. The amygdala, responsible for processing fear, might be hyperactive or overly sensitive in those with avoidant attachment, leading to a heightened sense of vulnerability and a readiness to withdraw at signs of emotional demands. Concurrently, the reward system, which governs feelings of pleasure from close social ties, might be less responsive. This combination creates a unique internal conflict: while part of you craves closeness, another stronger part resists it fiercely, all in a bid to protect you from potential emotional discomfort or pain.

Viewing avoidant attachment merely as a relational preference is a misunderstanding of its role as a survival mechanism. Developed in response to early life experiences where emotional needs were not adequately met, this attachment style is a form of emotional armor. In childhood, if expressing needs led to rejection or indifference, you might have learned to keep these needs to yourself and rely heavily on self-sufficiency. This coping strategy, once necessary for emotional survival, can become ingrained, persisting into adulthood even when it no longer serves you.

Understanding the depths of avoidant attachment is crucial, not only for self-awareness but also as a first step toward healing. Recognizing that your behaviors have deep-seated roots can be liberating. It offers a framework to understand your actions and feelings, but more importantly, it provides a roadmap for change. In the following pages, we will explore how you can navigate these waters, gradually easing the fears that keep you at arm's length from more profound connections.

Identifying Dismissive-Avoidant Behaviors in Daily Life

Certain behaviors in your day-to-day life might subtly signal your dismissive-avoidant attachment style, though they can often pass unnoticed, masquerading as mere personal quirks or preferences. For instance, consider how you might feel compelled to check your phone repeatedly during a close, emotional conversation or how you might steer discussions with friends towards superficial topics, avoiding any delve into deeper emotional territories. These are not random habits; they are symptomatic of a dismissive-avoidant attachment style, where emotional withdrawal and a pronounced reliance on self-sufficiency dominate.

These behaviors, while protective, often manifest distinctly in different types of relationships. In romantic partnerships, you might find yourself hesitating to commit or creating emotional distance by focusing excessively on work or hobbies whenever the relationship starts to deepen. This isn't because the partnership lacks importance; instead, it's a preemptive strike against the vulnerability that intimacy entails. With friends, the pattern might include consistently favoring digital communication over face-to-face interactions, as this can offer a sense of control and emotional safeguarding. Within the family, especially in relationships that historically might have felt invasive or overwhelming, you might notice a tendency to limit visits or phone calls, scheduling them as if they were formal appointments, all in an effort to manage the closeness on your terms. Similarly, interactions with colleagues are likely kept strictly professional, with any personal sharing forming part of a well-considered strategy rather than a spontaneous emotional connection.

Your self-perception as someone with an avoidant attachment style often centers around a strong identification with independence. You likely view yourself as self-reliant, capable, and most comfortable when in control of your emotional environment. This self-image is comforting, as it aligns with societal values that often glorify self-sufficiency. However, beneath this surface, there might be a less recognized longing for connection that feels too risky to acknowledge fully. This dichotomy between your outward behavior and inner desires can sometimes leave you feeling misunderstood by others, who may only see your independence and not your concealed need for closeness.

Recognizing these behaviors in yourself is the first crucial step toward change. It begins with honest self-reflection, which can be challenging given that these patterns have likely served as your emotional armor for years. Start by observing your reactions in various relational contexts. How do you feel when someone asks for more of your time or emotional energy? Anxious? Irritated and compelled to retreat? Documenting these reactions can be insightful. You might use a journal to track instances when you withdraw or deflect in relationships. Reflect on what triggers these responses—perhaps a particular tone of voice, a type of question, or even a specific person.

Over time, patterns will emerge, providing clarity on how your avoidant attachment style shapes your interactions. This will help guide you toward which aspects of your behavior might be ripe for transformation. This self-awareness is a powerful tool, illuminating the path from avoidance to connection, from independence to interdependence, where relationships are not just manageable but enriching and fully embraced.

The Impact of Childhood Experiences on Attachment Style

The roots of our attachment styles are often traced back to the tender years of childhood, where the foundational dynamics of our relationships with caregivers pave the pathways of our emotional landscapes. In these early interactions, the stage is set not on grand theatrical scales but in the quiet moments—the response to a cry, the comfort of a hug, the steadiness of a routine. For those who develop an avoidant attachment style, these moments often tell a story of emotional unavailability and the adaptive responses that ensue.

The emotional availability of caregivers is critical in the development of attachment styles. When a caregiver is consistently responsive, a child learns that the world is a safe place, that emotional expression is effective, and that their needs will be met. However, if a caregiver is emotionally distant, inconsistently available, or overly intrusive, the child must adapt. For those who grow into avoidant attachment styles, this often means learning to minimize or suppress their emotional needs. It's not that the need for comfort and emotional connection isn't there; instead, it becomes buried under layers of self-protection. This adaptation is a survival strategy in an environment where overt emotional expression does not reliably bring comfort or may even bring discomfort.

Children are incredibly adaptive, adjusting their behaviors based on their environment. In the case of avoidant attachment, the adaptation often involves developing a high degree of self-sufficiency. On the surface, this might appear as a strength, and in many ways, it can be. However, when self-sufficiency is born out of the necessity to protect oneself from the unpredictable emotional responses of caregivers, it can lead to a dismissal of one's emotional needs. These children learn to rely heavily on themselves, not necessarily because they don't have emotional needs, but because they have learned that not depending on others emotionally is a less painful path.

The trauma of these early experiences leaves a significant imprint on how individuals perceive and respond to closeness and vulnerability. If expressing needs once led to rejection or indifference, the memory of these experiences, often held more in the body than consciously remembered, can trigger a swift shutdown in adult relationships. The body remembers, even if the mind does not always make the connection. As adults, closeness may be equated subconsciously with danger, vulnerability with weakness, and independence with safety. These are the emotional imprints that shape the relational world of someone with an avoidant attachment style.

The long-term impact of these foundational experiences is profound. They shape not only how individuals approach relationships but also their self-perception. Adults with avoidant attachment styles often see themselves as strong and independent, priding themselves on not needing others in ways that seem to make others vulnerable. Yet, this strength is usually a mask for the fear that if they were to show their true needs, they would be met with the same inconsistency or coldness they experienced as children. This belief system can make it incredibly challenging to form deep, lasting relationships that require mutual vulnerability and dependence.

Recognizing the influence of these early experiences is an important step in breaking the cycle of avoidant attachment. Understanding that one's relational patterns are not fixed traits but adaptive responses to past conditions can open the door to compassion for oneself and a willingness to explore new ways of relating. The possibility of change begins with understanding, seeing the link between past and present, and recognizing that different responses might now be possible. This insight does not erase the challenges but illuminates a path through them, offering hope that the patterns learned in childhood need not dictate the pattern of one's future relationships.

A Brain's Perspective on Emotional Detachment

Understanding avoidant attachment necessitates a deep dive into the intricate workings of our brains, particularly how various regions and neurochemical activities influence our attachment behaviors and emotional regulations. Central to this exploration are the amygdala and prefrontal cortex—two brain regions that play pivotal roles in how we process emotions and manage relationships.

The amygdala, often referred to as the alarm bell of the brain, regulates our responses to perceived threats and safety. For someone with an avoidant attachment style, the amygdala's heightened vigilance can mean that signals of emotional closeness trigger a subconscious alert, prompting a swift withdrawal into emotional safety. This response is not merely a whim but a deeply ingrained protective mechanism. Conversely, the prefrontal cortex, which governs rational thinking and emotional regulation, often works to moderate these alarms, attempting to assess whether the threat is real and how best to respond. However, in avoidant attachment, there is frequently a disconnect or imbalance between these two regions. The result? A tendency to over-prioritize independence and self-reliance, often at the cost of fulfilling relationships.

Neurochemical factors also play a significant role in shaping our attachment styles. Neurotransmitters like dopamine and serotonin significantly influence how we experience pleasure and pain, rewards and punishments. Dopamine, often dubbed the 'feel-good' hormone, is crucial in the reward pathways of the brain. It reinforces behaviors that give us pleasure and helps us form habits around them. For individuals with avoidant attachment, the dopamine response to emotional closeness may be blunted. They do not experience the same reward from close relationships that others might, making these connections feel less compelling, even uncomfortable. Serotonin, another critical neurotransmitter, helps regulate mood and anxiety. Imbalances in serotonin levels can exacerbate feelings of anxiety and fear, which may further discourage someone with an avoidant style from seeking out and maintaining close emotional ties.

The body's response to stress, orchestrated by the hypothalamic-pituitary-adrenal (HPA) axis, is another critical element in understanding avoidant attachment. The HPA axis controls your reaction to stress and regulates a handful of body processes such as digestion, the immune system, mood and emotions, and energy storage. In moments of stress, the body releases cortisol, a hormone designed to help you cope with the threat. In the context of attachment, if early experiences taught you that closeness equals emotional danger, your HPA axis might be quick to launch into action when potential emotional stress appears—like when a relationship starts to deepen. This can make maintaining close, personal relationships challenging, as your body is essentially in a heightened state of alert, ready to defend against what it perceives as a threat to your emotional independence.

However, amidst these complexities, there is a beacon of hope in the concept of neuroplasticity. Neuroplasticity refers to the brain's power to be aware of itself by creating new neural connections throughout life. This means that the brain is not static but adaptable; it can learn new ways of being and relating. Understanding this can be incredibly empowering for someone with an avoidant attachment style. It implies that the ways of connecting and forming attachments are not fixed. With conscious effort and persistence, you can encourage your brain to favor healthier pathways, fostering closeness and intimacy rather than withdrawing from it. This might involve gradually exposing yourself to emotional closeness in a controlled and safe manner, effectively training your brain to understand that intimacy is not a threat but a source of joy and fulfillment.

The journey towards altering deep-seated attachment behaviors is undeniably complex and requires a nuanced understanding of the interplay between brain functions, neurochemicals, and stress responses. However, the knowledge that our brains are capable of change is a powerful motivator. It provides a scientific foundation for hope and transformation, reinforcing the idea that with the right strategies and support, moving towards more secure and fulfilling ways of relating is within reach. This understanding is not just theoretical; it's a practical tool that you can use to reshape your attachment style and enhance your relationships. As we continue to explore these themes, remember that each step forward is a step that takes you closer to a more connected and emotionally rewarding life.

Misconceptions About Avoidant Attachment Debunked

Understanding avoidant attachment often means navigating through a thicket of misconceptions that obscure the true nature of this attachment style. One of the most common of these is the idea that avoidant attachment is merely a phase or a mood that someone can simply "snap out of." This misinterpretation minimizes the complexity of avoidant attachment, which is, in fact, a persistent pattern of interacting with others that profoundly influences an individual's approach to relationships. It's not something that one can switch off like a light; rather, it's woven into the very fabric of how they connect with others, shaped by years of conditioning and experience.

Another widespread misunderstanding revolves around notions of love and intimacy. There exists a persistent belief among individuals with avoidant attachment that showing vulnerability is a sign of weakness, that it might lead to exploitation or hurt. This belief system can make the idea of opening up seem fraught with danger, a risk not worth taking. However, vulnerability is not a weakness but a strength to nurture. It allows for deeper, more meaningful connections, fostering a shared understanding and intimacy that can significantly enhance the quality of relationships. Acknowledging and embracing vulnerability as a strength requires a significant shift in perspective, one that sees emotional openness not as a liability but as a pathway to more fulfilling interactions.

The myth of permanence is another area fraught with misunderstanding. Many hold the belief that once an avoidant, their patterns of attachment are fixed and unchangeable. However, research in neuroplasticity and various therapeutic interventions tells us this is not the case. The fact that the brain's ability can adapt and create new neural connections means that change is always possible. Therapeutic approaches, particularly those focused on attachment theories, can provide strategies and insights that help individuals reframe their approach to relationships and gradually adopt more secure attachment behaviors.

The function of emotional distancing as a self-protection mechanism is often misunderstood as well. For those with avoidant attachment, maintaining a distance is not about a lack of interest or disdain towards others. Rather, it is a protective strategy developed to guard against the perceived threats of closeness. Recognizing this as a protective, rather than antisocial or cold, mechanism can change how individuals view their own behaviors and the behaviors of others, fostering a greater understanding and patience for the underlying fears that drive these actions. Additionally, the notion that individuals with avoidant attachment do not feel emotions deeply is another significant misconception. The reality is often quite the contrary; many avoidantly attached individuals experience deep emotions but may have learned to suppress or not express them due to past experiences. This internalization of emotion should not be confused with a lack of emotional capacity or depth. Rather, it's a learned behavior that can be unlearned, allowing for a more open and expressive emotional life.

The value of independence also tends to be misconstrued. While self-reliance is indeed a strength, when overemphasized to the detriment of interpersonal connections, it can lead to isolation and loneliness. Independence in balance with interdependence can lead to healthier, more sustainable relationships where both self-sufficiency and mutual support coexist. Striking this balance is vital, allowing for both personal growth and the nurturing of close relationships.

Finally, it is crucial to consider the emotional and relational costs of maintaining strict avoidant strategies. While these behaviors may feel safe, they often lead to a sense of loneliness and a persistent unfulfillment in relationships. The cost of such avoidance can be high, impacting not only the individual's well-being but also their potential for experiencing deep, meaningful connections with others. Recognizing these costs can often be the catalyst needed for someone to seek change and move towards a more engaged and open relational style that can dramatically enhance both their own life and the lives of those around them.

Understanding these misconceptions and addressing them directly is essential for anyone looking to shift away from an avoidant attachment style. By debunking these myths, new pathways open up—opportunities for growth, connection, and a fuller engagement with the relational world. Embracing these truths can be transformative, offering a new lens through which to view relationships and one's own capacity for change.

Chapter 2
Recognizing Avoidant Tendencies

Picture yourself at a bustling social gathering: the room brims with laughter and lively conversations, yet there's a part of you that remains distant, as if behind a glass wall. You interact, perhaps even smile, but the deeper the conversation threatens to tread, the more you feel an intuitive pull to retreat into your shell. This isn't just shyness; it's a nuanced dance of engagement and withdrawal, a hallmark of avoidant attachment. In this chapter, we delve into the spectrum of avoidant behaviors, understanding their variability and how they manifest in your relationships, guiding you to a deeper self-awareness and paving the way for personal growth.

The Spectrum of Avoidance: From Mild to Severe

Avoidant attachment, much like a color spectrum, doesn't present itself in a singular form but rather spans a continuum from mild to severe. It's crucial to understand that this is not a one-size-fits-all label. Some individuals might show only subtle signs of avoidance, such as hesitancy in sharing personal feelings. In contrast, others might actively push people away or end relationships prematurely to avoid emotional discomfort. This spectrum is influenced by a variety of factors, including early childhood experiences, past traumas, and even the individual's inherent temperament. Recognizing this variability is the first step in understanding that your way of relating to others is not merely a personal choice or preference but a complex interplay of many underlying elements.

The point you occupy on this spectrum profoundly influences how you behave in relationships. If your avoidance is mild, you might still maintain close relationships, but perhaps with an undercurrent of emotional distance that others find difficult to bridge. On the more severe end, you might avoid close relationships altogether, possibly perceiving them as unnecessary or too risky. This can manifest in behaviors such as declining invitations to social events, ghosting people after a few interactions, or even in the realm of romantic relationships, where commitment may feel like a cage rather than a comfort.

Determining where you fall on this avoidance spectrum requires honest self-reflection. Consider how you react when someone tries to get close to you emotionally. Do you find yourself diverting the conversation, using humor to deflect serious topics, or feeling the urge to distance yourself from others physically? Reflecting on your past and current relationships can also offer insights. Think about your significant relationships: what patterns do you see? Are there repeated instances where you felt compelled to leave relationships when they got too close for comfort? Noticing these patterns is not an exercise in self-judgment but a step towards self-understanding.

Understanding where you stand on the spectrum of avoidant attachment is not just about self-awareness; it's about setting the stage for meaningful change. If you recognize mild avoidance tendencies, your strategies might involve gradually opening up to emotional risks, like sharing a personal story or expressing your feelings in a relationship. For those on the severe end, the approach might involve more foundational work, possibly with professional support, to explore and heal the deeper wounds that fuel your avoidance. In both cases, recognizing your position on the spectrum allows you to tailor your growth strategies effectively, ensuring they are not just general suggestions but personalized steps that resonate with your specific experiences and needs.

In navigating these insights, remember that self-awareness is a powerful tool. It illuminates the hidden corners of your attachment style, helping you understand not just how you engage in relationships, but why. This understanding is your ally, a beacon that guides you through the fog of avoidance toward a horizon of more fulfilling connections. As you move forward, hold onto this knowledge, let it inform your choices and behaviors in relationships, and watch as the landscape of your emotional world transforms, revealing potentials you might never have imagined possible.

Self-Assessment: Are You Subconsciously Avoiding Intimacy?

When we talk about the fear of intimacy, we are referring to an apprehension or hesitance to open oneself fully to another person due to the potential emotional risks involved. This fear typically manifests across three dimensions: thoughts, emotions, and behaviors. In your mind, it might echo as a series of warnings—"Don't get too close," or "They might hurt you." Emotionally, it can feel like a constant battle between the desire for closeness and the urge to shield yourself from potential hurt and disappointment. Behaviorally, it often results in actions that create distance on one's terms, whether through delaying responses to messages, opting out of deeper conversations, or even ending relationships when they start to feel too close.

Recognizing these signs in yourself can be challenging but incredibly enlightening. Here are several indicators that might suggest a tendency toward avoiding intimacy:

1. Reluctance to Share Personal Information: You might find it hard to share personal details or feelings, even with those you've known for a long time.
2. Preference for Superficial Interactions: You may prefer interactions that skim the surface, steering clear of deep emotional exchanges.
3. Physical and Emotional Withdrawal: This could involve pulling away from physical closeness or shutting down emotionally when conversations venture into more intimate territory.
4. Sabotaging Relationships: Perhaps you find reasons why relationships won't work out, focusing on flaws or differences as justifications for distancing yourself.
5. Overemphasis on Independence: While being independent is healthy, using it as a shield against any form of reliance on others might be a sign of avoiding intimacy.

To better understand your behaviors and feelings towards intimacy, consider reflecting on these questions:

- When was the last time you openly shared your feelings with someone, and how did it make you feel?
- Can you think of a moment when you purposely kept someone at arm's length? What prompted this action?
- How do you react internally when someone expresses a desire to be closer to you emotionally?
- Are there patterns in your past relationships in which you ended things or pulled back when they became too serious or emotionally involved?

Acknowledging these tendencies is more than just an exercise in self-awareness—it's a transformative act that sets the stage for growth. It allows you to see where your protective measures might be hindering deeper connections, providing a clearer picture of what changes might be beneficial for you. This acknowledgment is not about self-blame but about understanding and compassion for oneself. It's recognizing that your behaviors have been protective mechanisms, not flaws or failures.

Beginning to work on these aspects of your life doesn't mean an immediate overhaul of who you are; it's about making incremental changes that allow you to experience deeper connections without overwhelming yourself. It's about setting boundaries that feel safe but are also permeable enough to let others in. This gradual opening can be challenging, but it also opens up a new realm of possibilities for relationships that are full of emotional depth and mutual understanding. As you navigate this process, remember that each small step is part of a more significant progression toward a life where intimacy is not something to be feared but embraced as a source of joy and strength.

Deactivation Strategies: How You Unknowingly Sabotage Connections

In the landscape of avoidant attachment, deactivation strategies serve as a sort of psychological immune system, kicking into action whenever the threat of emotional exposure becomes too imminent. These are the subconscious tactics you employ to maintain your comfort zone of emotional distance. For instance, you might find yourself rationalizing reasons to avoid spending time with someone who is showing interest in you, or you might focus on small imperfections in your friends or partners to emotionally justify your withdrawal from those relationships. Another common strategy is to downplay your feelings of affection or care, telling yourself and others that you "just aren't that into" someone who could potentially be a significant partner.

These mechanisms are not acts of deliberate coldness but rather protective measures developed over time. Often, they stem from early experiences where emotional vulnerability was met with pain, leading you to equate closeness with discomfort. This learned response is your psyche's way of defending itself; it's an attempt to control the environment by preventing others from getting too close. This self-protection can be so integrated into your behavior patterns that it feels completely natural, just another part of who you are.

Recognizing when you are employing these deactivation strategies is crucial for anyone looking to reshape their attachment behaviors. Awareness begins with close, mindful observation of your reactions in situations that invoke vulnerability. For example, after a date that went well, do you find yourself picking apart your date's behavior or characteristics, focusing on why they wouldn't be a good long-term match? When friends seek more profound emotional support, do you find reasons to remain busy or disengage? Observing these patterns without immediate judgment can be challenging but is essential in understanding your relational dynamics.

This awareness then opens the door to exploring healthier alternatives to these deactivation strategies. Instead of pulling away when a relationship starts to deepen, you might experiment with small steps toward openness and vulnerability. This doesn't mean oversharing or forcing intimacy; instead, it's about gradually letting your guard down at a pace that feels manageable. For example, if you're used to keeping conversations light, you might share a personal story or feeling relevant to the discussion. It's about making a conscious choice to stay engaged even when your instinct might be to step back.

Transitioning away from automatic deactivation requires patience and practice. It involves relearning how to handle vulnerability—not as a threat but as a bridge to deeper human connections. It means retraining your emotional responses, allowing yourself to experience closeness, and observing how it doesn't necessarily lead to the negative outcomes you might anticipate. This process can initially increase anxiety or discomfort because it challenges long-standing patterns. However, the more you practice these new behaviors, the more you reinforce the understanding within yourself that closeness can be safe, rewarding, and enriching.

This exploration of alternative ways to manage vulnerability not only enhances your ability to form and maintain satisfying relationships but also contributes to a broader emotional resilience. You begin to trust not just other people but also yourself and your ability to handle emotional situations. This trust is a crucial component of internal security, which supports a more secure attachment style. As you continue to engage with these new strategies, you gradually build a repertoire of responses that encourage connection rather than distance, fundamentally shifting the dynamics of your relationships toward something more open, mutual, and fulfilling.

Emotional Numbing: Signs and Solutions

In the quiet solitude of your own experiences, you might notice moments where feelings that should be vibrant and engaging seem distant or muted. This phenomenon, known as emotional numbing, is not uncommon, especially among those with an avoidant attachment style. It acts as a psychological buffer, a way to shield oneself from potential emotional distress by dulling the senses to both negative and positive emotions. You might recognize it as a persistent sense of detachment from your feelings or an inability to engage with joyful or sad occasions fully. For example, you may find yourself feeling indifferent during events that should be happy or fulfilling, such as a friend's wedding or a professional achievement. Alternatively, in situations that would typically elicit a strong emotional response, like a family conflict or a romantic breakup, you might notice a conspicuous absence of any profound emotional reaction.

This emotional detachment can significantly impact your relationships and your self-awareness. In relationships, it often manifests as a lack of emotional depth. Your friends, family, and partners might perceive you as cold or unfeeling, not because you don't have emotions but because you are not fully experiencing or expressing them. This may lead to misunderstandings and frustrations, as those close to you might feel rejected or undervalued, not realizing that your subconscious defenses are stifling your emotional responses. In terms of self-awareness, emotional numbing can prevent you from fully understanding your own needs and feelings. Without a clear connection to your emotional self, making decisions that truly resonate with your desires and needs becomes challenging, leading to a life that might feel unfulfilling or disconnected from your true self.

Combatting emotional numbing involves reconnecting with your emotional world. An effective strategy is to engage in activities that have historically sparked a sense of passion or excitement in you. This could involve creative pursuits like painting, writing, or playing music—activities that can help surface buried emotions in a safe and controlled environment. Alternatively, physical activities like hiking, dancing, or yoga can help reconnect your physical and emotional selves, as these activities stimulate not only your body but also your emotional awareness.

Another powerful approach is mindfulness meditation, which involves sitting silently and observing your thoughts and feelings without judgment. This practice can help you become more attuned to your emotions as they arise, rather than letting them pass unnoticed. Start with just a few minutes each day, and slowly increase the time as you become more comfortable with the practice. The key is consistency; the more regularly you practice mindfulness, the more likely you are to break through the barriers of emotional numbing.

Seeking professional help can also be a crucial step in addressing emotional numbing, especially if the disconnection feels deep-seated and persistent. Therapists specializing in attachment disorders can offer personalized strategies tailored to your specific experiences and needs. Therapy gives you a safe space to work through your emotions, understand their roots, and develop healthier ways to deal with them. Techniques like Cognitive Behavioral Therapy (CBT) or Eye Movement Desensitization and Reprocessing (EMDR) can be effective in dealing with the traumas that often underlie emotional numbing. These therapies help by reprocessing past traumas and changing the thought patterns that contribute to emotional detachment.

Engaging in these practices does not mean that you will overnight become a paragon of emotional expression. Instead, it's about gradually peeling back the layers of defense that have muted your emotional experiences. Each small step forward is a piece of the larger puzzle of your emotional well-being, contributing to a more vibrant emotional life. As you navigate these strategies, remember to be patient and kind to yourself. Emotional reconnection is a delicate process, one that requires time, consistency, and, most importantly, a willingness to engage with the full spectrum of your emotional experiences.

The Avoidant's Inner Dialogue: Understanding Your Thought Patterns

In the quiet moments when you're alone with your thoughts, what narratives play out in your mind? For those with an avoidant attachment style, these internal monologues often reinforce a fear of dependency and a dread of losing one's sense of self to the demands of a close relationship. You might catch yourself thinking, "If I let someone get too close, I'll lose my independence," or "Relationships are just too complicated and painful." These thought patterns are not just fleeting worries; they are deeply ingrained beliefs that can dictate how you navigate your emotional world, pushing you towards isolation even when part of you yearns for connection.

This internal conflict—the simultaneous craving for connection and inherent fear of closeness—is a defining struggle for individuals with avoidant attachment. On one hand, there's a natural human desire for warmth, affection, and companionship. On the other, there's a paralyzing fear that embracing these desires fully might lead to vulnerability and, ultimately, pain. This tug-of-war can create significant emotional turmoil, making it challenging to form and maintain healthy, satisfying relationships. The key to easing this conflict lies in addressing the negative beliefs that fuel your fears.

Challenging these negative beliefs starts with recognizing them. Begin by identifying the automatic thoughts that surface when you think about forming or deepening relationships. What do you tell yourself about your ability to maintain independence in a relationship? How do you perceive the intentions of others? Often, these thoughts are based on past experiences or deep-seated fears rather than the reality of the situation. By identifying these thought patterns, you can begin to question their validity and explore their origins, which is often the first step in transforming them.

Reframing these thought patterns involves constructing new, more positive narratives about relationships and your role in them. For instance, instead of thinking, "If I get close to someone, I'll lose my independence," you might reframe this thought to, "I can maintain my independence while also enjoying close relationships." This process of reframing is not about denying your feelings but rather about opening up to new, more constructive ways of viewing relationships that don't automatically equate closeness with loss of self.

To support these new narratives, engaging in positive self-talk can be incredibly beneficial. This might involve daily affirmations that reinforce your ability to be both independent and intimately connected. Phrases like "I am capable of maintaining my sense of self in relationships" or "I can manage closeness without compromise" can be powerful reminders of your capacity for change and growth. Repeating these affirmations regularly can help cement these positive beliefs in your mind, gradually reducing the impact of the negative patterns that have previously dictated your approach to relationships.

Additionally, mindfulness and thought observation techniques can be invaluable tools in this process. Mindfulness involves focusing on the present moment and observing your thoughts and feelings without judgment. This practice can help you become more aware of the negative thought patterns as they arise, giving you the chance to handle them proactively. Regular mindfulness practice, whether through meditation, mindful breathing, or simply taking a few moments each day to reflect quietly, can enhance your ability to catch and adjust these thoughts. The key is consistency; the more regularly you practice mindfulness, the more adept you become at recognizing and managing your avoidant tendencies.

By understanding and adjusting your inner dialogue, you lay the groundwork for more authentic and fulfilling relationships. This doesn't mean that the fear of closeness will disappear overnight, but rather that you develop greater agency in choosing how to respond to these fears. Each step in this process, from recognizing to reframing to reinforcing new beliefs, builds on the last, creating a foundation for lasting change. As you continue to explore and adjust your thought patterns, you may find that what once felt threatening now seems more manageable, opening up new possibilities for connection and closeness that previously felt out of reach.

In this chapter, we've explored the intricacies of the avoidant's inner dialogue, uncovering the common thought patterns that reinforce avoidant attachment and learning strategies to challenge and change these beliefs. By understanding the internal conflict that drives your avoidance and employing tools like positive self-talk and mindfulness, you can begin to reshape your approach to relationships and intimacy. As we move forward, remember that each step you take in understanding and transforming your thought patterns contributes to a broader journey toward emotional openness and more rewarding relationships.

Chapter 3

The Anatomy of Avoidant Relationships

Imagine finding yourself at the edge of a serene lake. The setting is perfect for a dive, yet there's a hesitance, a whisper of doubt that holds you back from experiencing the cool embrace of the water. This moment of pause, this interplay between desire and reluctance, mirrors the emotional landscape of those with an avoidant attachment style as they navigate the depths of romantic relationships. While the allure of intimacy beckons, the fear of losing oneself to the depths of emotional union often keeps one standing at the shore, toes dipped shallowly into the water.

Romantic Pitfalls: Navigating Love as an Avoidant

Navigating romantic relationships often presents a unique set of challenges for someone with an avoidant attachment style. The desire for deep, meaningful connection exists, but it's regularly overshadowed by the fear of what such connections might entail. It's akin to wanting to sail the seas of closeness yet fearing the potential storms of emotional demands and vulnerabilities. This juxtaposition leads to a common suite of challenges that can make romantic relationships feel like a treacherous domain.

One of the most significant hurdles is the fear of losing independence. For you, independence isn't just a lifestyle choice; it's a sanctuary, a vital part of your identity that offers safety and control. The thought of a relationship infringing upon this sanctuary can trigger a profound sense of unease. You might find yourself pulling away just when a relationship starts to deepen, a reflexive step back into the familiar territory of solitude. Addressing this fear begins with recognizing that independence and intimacy are not mutually exclusive. It involves redefining what being in a relationship means to you and understanding that a healthy relationship can actually support and enhance your independence rather than diminish it. Strategies here might include setting clear personal boundaries from the outset, communicating your needs openly, and choosing partners who respect and encourage your autonomy.

Building trust is another pivotal challenge. Trust involves vulnerability, a state that might feel inherently risky if your historical blueprint equates closeness with potential pain. However, trust is also the foundation upon which enduring relationships are built. Cultivating it requires a gradual approach, perhaps beginning with small confidences and working up to more significant shared vulnerabilities. It's about creating a series of positive experiences in the relationship that, over time, can help recalibrate your perceptions of intimacy. This slow build helps to foster a sense of safety, showing you that not all emotional risks result in pain and that there are profound joys and comforts in mutual trust.

Communicating needs effectively is also crucial, yet often complicated by an instinct to protect oneself from potential rejection or disappointment. You might struggle with expressing needs for fear of being too demanding or driving the other person away. However, clear communication is essential not only for meeting your needs but also for establishing transparency and mutual understanding in a relationship. Effective communication can be enhanced through practices like regular check-ins with your partner about the relationship, using direct "I" statements to express your feelings and needs directly, and actively listening to your partner's needs and concerns. These practices encourage a dialogue that respects both partners' needs, fostering a relationship where both feel heard and valued.

Navigating love as someone with an avoidant attachment style is not without its challenges, but it also holds the promise of profound growth and fulfillment. As you learn to balance your need for independence with the joys of close connection, to build trust gradually, and to communicate openly, you open up new possibilities for yourself in love—possibilities where relationships enrich your life, complement your independence, and offer new dimensions of joy and discovery. Each step forward in this domain is not just about enhancing your romantic relationships; it's about expanding your emotional repertoire and deepening your understanding of yourself and others. These are the steps that, taken together, can transform the very nature of your journey through love and intimacy, turning apprehension into exploration, and reluctance into readiness for the rich emotional landscapes that relationships offer.

The Avoidant in Friendships: Balancing Independence and Closeness

In the tapestry of social interactions, friendships hold a special place. They offer a spectrum of intimacies, from the casual acquaintance at a gym to the deep confidant whose history intertwines closely with one's own. For someone with an avoidant attachment style, the landscape of these relationships can be particularly complex. You might find yourself enjoying the company of friends, valuing their presence in your life, yet simultaneously feeling a barrier that prevents these relationships from deepening. This barrier isn't built from a lack of interest or affection, but rather from a subconscious guard against the vulnerabilities that closer friendships demand.

Navigating the dynamics of friendships often means managing a delicate balance between closeness and the preservation of your independence. The fear that deepening intimacy might lead to obligations that could infringe on your personal freedom can cause you to hold friends at arm's length. Social gatherings might be met with enthusiasm, but the private sharing of fears, hopes, or dreams during one-on-one interactions tends to trigger a step back, a retreat into the safe haven of solitude. This pattern not only restricts the depth of your relationships but can also leave your friends feeling perplexed or rejected, wondering why their attempts to grow closer seem to be met with resistance.

Establishing and maintaining healthy boundaries is important when navigating these waters. Boundaries shouldn't be barriers. Instead, they should serve as defined lines that both parties understand and respect, allowing for mutual comfort and the gradual deepening of trust. Effective boundary-setting begins with self-reflection—understanding what you're comfortable sharing and how much companionship you desire. It might mean being upfront with your friends about your needs for alone time or setting limits on how often and in what ways you feel comfortable engaging. Communicate these boundaries clearly and kindly, ensuring that they're understood not as rejections but as frameworks within which a more trusting and comfortable relationship can evolve.

Actively investing in friendships while maintaining this sense of self involves a conscious engagement that respects both your boundaries and the needs of your friends. It's about quality rather than quantity. You might not be the friend who's always there, but you can be the friend who's fully present in the moments you choose to share. This might look like committing to regular but spaced-out coffee dates where real conversations can happen or joining a group activity that aligns with a shared interest, providing a natural setting for connection that doesn't feel forced or threatening to your autonomy.

Recognizing the value of deeper friendships is an essential part of this equation. While independence is a significant aspect of your personality, human connections, even those that push you slightly out of your comfort zone, bring unique joys and supports that are hard to replicate in solitude. These relationships can be mirrors, reflecting aspects of yourself you may not see, fortresses giving strength in times of struggle, and playgrounds that offer joy and relaxation. Embracing the value in these connections requires a shift in perspective, seeing them not as threats to your autonomy but as enrichments to your life, adding layers of color and dimension to your personal journey.

Navigating friendships as someone with an avoidant attachment style isn't about transforming into a social butterfly or altering the core of who you are. Instead, it's about expanding your ability to engage with others in ways that honor both your need for independence and your capacity for closeness. It's about building bridges at your own pace, establishing connections that respect your boundaries, and gradually recognizing the profound ways in which friendships can enhance and beautify your life. As you explore these dynamics, each step forward enriches your understanding of yourself and others, weaving a richer, more colorful social tapestry that supports and delights.

Family Dynamics: The Role of Avoidant Attachment

In the intricate web of family relationships, the threads of attachment styles weave profound patterns that influence interactions and emotional exchanges. For those with an avoidant attachment style, these patterns often manifest as a delicate dance of engagement and retreat, where the fear of losing autonomy intersects with familial obligations and expectations. Understanding how your avoidant attachment affects these family dynamics can provide insightful perspectives, paving the way for more harmonious interactions and perhaps even healing.

The family dynamic for someone with avoidant attachment often mirrors their early experiences with caregivers. Suppose those early interactions taught self-reliance at the expense of emotional support. In that case, you might find yourself replicating these patterns in adult family relationships, maintaining a safe emotional distance even from those closest to you. This distancing can manifest as reluctance to participate in family gatherings, hesitance to share personal achievements or challenges, or even in the subtler realms of failing to seek support during tough times. Your family might perceive this as aloofness or indifference when, in reality, it's a protective mechanism deeply ingrained from childhood.

Navigating the complex expectations and pressures of family life without compromising one's emotional needs is especially challenging. Families often operate on an implied set of norms and rules, and deviations from these can lead to misunderstandings or conflict. For you, managing these expectations might mean setting clear, compassionate boundaries that help your family understand your need for space without viewing it as a rejection. It could involve explicitly stating your comfort levels around participation in family events or discussing how you prefer to communicate, whether that's limiting phone calls to certain times of the day or preferring texts over spontaneous visits. These discussions aren't just logistical; they're about reshaping how your family interacts with you, fostering an environment where your needs are recognized and respected.

Healing strained family relationships often requires revisiting and sometimes revising the narratives that have defined these relationships. If historical interactions were marked by misunderstandings or emotional distance, introducing new ways of communicating can be transformative. Start by acknowledging past patterns and expressing a desire to change these dynamics for better mutual understanding. This might mean initiating conversations about how past behaviors made you feel and exploring how you and your family members can support each other more effectively. Remember, healing is not about assigning blame but about opening up new channels of empathy and understanding. It's a process that can gradually replace old wounds with new, healthier interactions.

Creating healthy boundaries with family members is perhaps one of the most crucial steps in this process. Boundaries allow you to love your family while still honoring your need for independence. Start by identifying what aspects of family interactions feel overwhelming or intrusive. Perhaps it's the expectation to always be available or pressure to conform to family roles that don't fit your true self. Once these areas are identified, communicate your needs clearly. For instance, if unplanned visits feel invasive, you might request that family members call before coming over. If constant questioning about personal life feels overwhelming, set a boundary around the types of questions you are willing to engage with. Effective boundaries are those that are stated clearly, upheld consistently, and adjusted as needed, allowing for a relationship dynamic that respects both your autonomy and your family's desire for closeness.

In navigating the complexities of family dynamics as someone with an avoidant attachment style, the goal is not to overhaul your personality but to create a balance that respects both your need for independence and your family's need for connection. This balance doesn't come overnight; it evolves through continuous effort, open communication, and a deep commitment to understanding both your own emotional landscape and that of your family members. As you engage in this process, you may find that the family dynamics, which once seemed like a minefield of obligations and misunderstandings, begin to transform into a more supportive and understanding network, reflecting a new pattern of interaction where your needs and those of your family are in greater harmony. This shift not only enhances your relationships within the family but also enriches your overall emotional well-being, providing a firmer foundation from which to engage with the world around you.

The Anxious-Avoidant Trap: Understanding the Push and Pull

In the tapestry of relationship dynamics, few patterns are as simultaneously complex and common as the anxious-avoidant trap. This dynamic unfolds when one partner's anxious attachment behaviors trigger the avoidant tendencies in the other, creating a cycle of push and pull that can be as frustrating as it is painful. The anxious partner, in their quest for closeness, often engages in behaviors that feel overwhelming to the avoidant partner, who then pulls away in a need for space. This withdrawal then triggers more anxiety and clinging behaviors from the anxious partner, setting the cycle to repeat. Understanding this pattern is vital, not just for identifying it, but for comprehending why it's such a prevalent dynamic among couples.

The trap typically ensnares partners because it plays directly into the core fears and responses of both attachment styles. For the anxious partner, the avoidant's withdrawal confirms their fears of abandonment and unworthiness, leading to heightened efforts to secure affection and reassurance. For the avoidant partner, the anxious partner's attempts at closeness can feel like threats to their independence and self-sufficiency, sparking a retreat into more solitary, emotionally detached behaviors. This interplay, without intervention, can become a steady dance of distress and withdrawal, leaving both partners feeling misunderstood, unfulfilled, and often exhausted by the relationship.

The emotional toll of this dynamic on both partners can be profound. Anxious partners may feel perpetually insecure and doubtful of their partner's love, leading to behaviors that can be perceived as needy or controlling. They live in a near-constant state of emotional turmoil, where moments of closeness are interspersed with intense fears of rejection. Avoidant partners, on the other hand, may feel that their personal space is being invaded and their independence curtailed, leading them to become distant, a state that can provoke guilt for their emotional unavailability and frustration at their partner's perceived clinginess. This push and pull can strain the relationship to its breaking points, often manifesting in recurrent arguments, emotional distance, and, in some cases, separation.

Navigating out of the anxious-avoidant trap requires a concerted effort from both partners to understand and adapt their attachment behaviors. For the avoidant partner, this might involve recognizing and gently challenging their impulses to withdraw. This could mean consciously deciding to stay present during emotionally charged conversations instead of retreating or expressing their need for space in ways that reassure the anxious partner of their commitment and affection. For the anxious partner, this might mean working on self-soothing techniques that allow them to manage their anxiety without seeking constant validation from their partner. It also involves recognizing the triggers that activate their anxious attachment behaviors and communicating these in a way that invites support rather than demanding reassurance.

Moving towards a more secure attachment in the relationship involves fostering an environment of open communication, mutual understanding, and patience. Both partners need to be willing to explore the roots of their attachment styles—often tied to early relationship experiences with caregivers—and how these influence their expectations and behaviors in the relationship. Therapy, either individually or as a couple, has proven to be an invaluable tool in this process. A trained therapist can assist you in unpacking the complex emotions and patterns at play, providing strategies to disrupt the cycle and build a more secure, supportive bond.

Building a relationship where both people feel secure and valued might involve setting new patterns of interaction. This could include establishing routines that ensure quality time together, creating rituals of connection such as a nightly check-in or morning coffee together, and consistently acknowledging and appreciating each other's efforts in the relationship. It's about small, consistent actions that build trust and intimacy over time, allowing both partners to feel more secure not just with each other but in their understanding of themselves.

As you and your partner undertake this work, remember that progress often comes in waves—moments of breakthrough can be followed by periods of struggle as old patterns resurface. Patience and commitment to the process are crucial. With time and effort, moving out of the anxious-avoidant trap and towards a more secure attachment becomes not just a possibility but a likely reality, opening up a new chapter of mutual growth and deeper connection.

Professional Relationships: Achieving Connection Without Vulnerability

In the realm of professional life, where the lines between personal and impersonal often blur, navigating relationships can be uniquely challenging for someone with an avoidant attachment style. The workplace demands a level of interaction and cooperation that might feel intrusive or demanding, yet it also necessitates a degree of detachment appropriate to a professional setting. Balancing these dynamics involves understanding how to establish professional boundaries that allow for meaningful, yet not overly personal, connections with colleagues.

Professional boundaries serve as the frameworks within which you interact with colleagues and superiors. They help define what is considered appropriate in terms of personal sharing, emotional support, and even physical space. For someone who leans towards avoidant attachment, these boundaries are often rigid, a protective measure to prevent the professional environment from becoming a source of emotional discomfort. However, overly rigid boundaries can keep you from forming the kinds of collegial relationships that enhance teamwork and facilitate career advancement. Striking a balance means setting boundaries that protect your comfort level while still allowing for a degree of emotional connection that can humanize workplace interactions. This could mean participating in team-building activities that feel comfortable, sharing professional achievements or challenges with colleagues, or simply engaging more openly in everyday conversations without crossing into personal territory that feels too exposed.

Avoidance in professional settings often manifests in ways that can subtly undermine career progression. You might decline leadership roles for fear of increased interpersonal demands, or you might avoid networking events that could lead to meaningful connections, viewing them as emotionally taxing rather than professionally beneficial. This kind of avoidance can limit your visibility and opportunities for advancement. Recognizing how your attachment style influences your professional behavior is the first step toward modifying these patterns. It involves a conscious decision to participate in professional activities that you might typically avoid, assessing realistically rather than reflexively the emotional cost versus the potential career benefit. This doesn't mean overhauling your natural tendencies overnight but rather making incremental adjustments that can gradually expand your professional engagement without overwhelming your comfort threshold.

Building a professional network that feels safe and supportive is crucial in this context. Start by identifying colleagues who respect your need for emotional space and who share professional values or goals. These individuals can form the nucleus of a network that feels both supportive and non-intrusive. From here, you can gradually extend your network, connecting with others through professional collaborations, conferences, or social media platforms like LinkedIn, where interactions can be controlled and predictable. Building this network involves regular but manageable interactions that don't feel forced or overly personal, allowing you to expand your professional relationships at a pace that doesn't trigger your avoidant tendencies.

Encouraging authenticity within professional boundaries is perhaps one of the most effective ways to foster genuine connections in the workplace. Authenticity involves bringing your true self to your professional interactions and aligning your actions and words with your genuine thoughts and feelings. For people with an avoidant attachment style, this may seem overwhelming, as it requires a level of openness that feels vulnerable. However, authenticity doesn't require profound personal disclosures; instead, it involves being genuine in your professional interactions, expressing your true opinions on work matters, or sharing your professional ambitions and ideas. This level of authenticity can significantly enhance your relationships at work, making interactions more engaging and fulfilling without crossing into personal vulnerability that feels uncomfortable.

Navigating professional relationships as someone with an avoidant attachment style involves a delicate balance of engaging without overexposing and participating without losing one's sense of safety. By establishing clear professional boundaries, gradually reducing avoidance behaviors, actively building a supportive network, and fostering authenticity within appropriate limits, you can create a professional life that is both successful and comfortable. This approach not only enhances your work experience but also contributes to a more balanced sense of self, one that can navigate the complexities of professional relationships with confidence and ease.

Solitude vs. Loneliness: Reconciling the Need for Space

In the quiet moments you carve out for yourself, away from the clamor of social interactions, there lies a profound opportunity for personal growth and introspection. This is the essence of solitude—an intentional state of being alone where you find a sense of peace and self-fulfillment. However, it's crucial to distinguish this enriching solitude from the pangs of loneliness, which can often masquerade as a similar experience but with vastly different emotional impacts. Solitude involves a deliberate choice to be alone for rejuvenation and reflection. At the same time, loneliness is characterized by a feeling of emptiness and isolation, an unwanted separation from others that can lead to sadness or despair.

The value of alone time is immense, particularly for someone with an avoidant attachment style. It offers a sanctuary where the pressures of emotional demands can be set aside and where the self can be explored without the distractions of constant interaction. This time is not about avoidance but about self-discovery and rejuvenation. It allows for activities that you might find nurturing or creatively stimulating—reading, writing, walking in nature, or practicing mindfulness and meditation. These activities not only enrich your sense of self but also provide the mental and emotional space necessary to process your experiences and emotions at your own pace, without the external pressure to react or explain your feelings.

However, the challenge arises when the line between comforting solitude and creeping loneliness begins to blur. It's possible to slide from using solitude as a healthy coping mechanism to finding yourself mired in loneliness without clear distinction. Addressing this slide requires mindfulness and honesty about your emotional state. Recognize the signs of loneliness perhaps an underlying sadness, a sense of something missing, or a feeling of disconnection not just from others but from yourself. When these feelings surface, it's crucial to challenge your natural inclination to withdraw further gently. Instead, consider reaching out to friends or family, not necessarily for lengthy interactions but for meaningful connection, like a quick chat or a shared activity that doesn't feel overwhelming but reminds you that you are part of a wider community.

Balancing solitude and socialization is a delicate art. It involves listening to your needs and recognizing when your scales are tipping too far toward isolation. Creating a schedule can sometimes help maintain this balance. Allocate specific times for solitude that allow you to engage in personal activities that you enjoy and find stimulating. Equally, carve out time for social activities that you find enjoyable and fulfilling with people who understand and respect your need for space. This balance might not look the same every day or every week; it's about making adjustments based on your ongoing emotional landscape, which can shift and change just like the weather.

This dynamic balance between solitude and socialization is not just about maintaining emotional health; it's about enriching your life experience. It allows you to enjoy the benefits of both worlds—using solitude for personal growth and using social interactions for emotional and psychological enrichment. As you navigate this balance, you continuously learn more about yourself—your needs, your boundaries, and your capacity for connection. This learning is a profound aspect of personal development, one that fosters a deeper understanding of who you are and how you relate to the world around you.

As this chapter closes, reflect on the interplay between solitude and loneliness in your life. Recognize the value of each state and the signals that might indicate a shift from one to the other. Consider how you might use both solitude and socialization as tools for personal growth and emotional well-being. Looking ahead, the journey continues to explore more ways to enhance your understanding of attachment styles and their impact on your life, ensuring each step you take is informed and intentional, leading towards a more connected existence.

Chapter 4
The Power of Self-Awareness

In the quiet solitude of your early morning or late-night moments, have you ever caught yourself wondering why you react the way you do in certain situations, especially when it comes to relationships? Perhaps there's a part of you that's curious about the patterns you seem to fall into repeatedly, almost as if by a script that you didn't write but somehow can't stop following. This chapter is about turning that script over in your hands, examining it under the light of self-awareness, and beginning to pen your own revisions. It's about building a bridge between your actions and your inner world, using tools that illuminate rather than judge, that explore rather than suppress.

Mindfulness Practices to Observe Avoidant Behaviors

Mindfulness, often visualized as the serene practice of meditation, holds profound implications far beyond its tranquil appearance, particularly for those grappling with avoidant attachment styles. At its core, mindfulness revolves around being present in the moment and being fully aware of your thoughts, feelings, and surroundings without succumbing to automatic judgments or reactions. This practice is especially relevant if you find yourself retreating in relationships or struggling with intimacy. It offers a way to slow down the rapid-fire responses that often lead to withdrawal, giving you space to choose how you want to engage with others and yourself.

The essence of mindfulness lies in its capacity to help you observe your behaviors and thoughts without criticism. This non-judgmental stance is crucial because it shifts how you relate to your avoidant behaviors. Typically, these behaviors might trigger self-criticism or shame—a cycle that only reinforces the desire to withdraw. Mindfulness changes the script, inviting curiosity instead of judgment. For instance, when you notice an urge to pull away from a partner or friend, mindfulness encourages you to acknowledge this reaction simply as information—neither good nor bad. This stance can be incredibly freeing, as it allows you to explore these reactions as part of your emotional landscape without the added pressure of having to correct or change them immediately.

Integrating mindfulness into your daily routine can start with simple exercises explicitly tailored to recognize and pause avoidant behaviors. One effective practice is the 'mindful check-in'—several times throughout your day, especially during interactions that typically trigger your avoidance, take a moment to assess your emotional state. How are you feeling? What thoughts are running through your mind? Are your muscles tense? Are you preparing to end the conversation or make an excuse to leave? This check-in shouldn't take more than a minute or two, but it can provide invaluable insights into your habitual responses and the triggers that activate them.

Breaking the cycle of avoidance through mindfulness involves using the awareness cultivated in these check-ins to make different choices. For example, suppose you notice during a check-in that you're feeling overwhelmed in a social situation and are preparing to retreat. In that case, you might choose instead to communicate your feelings to the person you're with or decide to stay another five minutes before deciding whether to leave. These decisions might seem small, but they represent powerful acts of choice rather than reflexive reactions. Over time, these choices can begin to reshape your automatic responses to fear of intimacy, gradually teaching you that closeness does not always lead to discomfort or loss.

Incorporating mindfulness into your daily life enhances your self-awareness and provides tools to manage avoidant tendencies more effectively. You could set reminders to practice mindful breathing for a few minutes each day, perhaps before meetings or social events that typically trigger avoidant behaviors. You might also engage in a daily practice of mindfulness meditation, using guided sessions from apps or online platforms to help maintain focus and consistency. The key is regular practice—like any skill, mindfulness gets stronger and more valuable the more you practice it.

As you continue to engage with these mindfulness practices, you might start to notice subtle shifts in your interactions and your responses to intimacy. Perhaps the edges of your anxiety soften, making it easier to stay present with others. Or you might find yourself more willing to express your needs and boundaries, knowing that you can handle the vulnerability those conversations require. These changes are signs of the profound impact mindfulness can have, not just on your relationships with others but on your relationship with yourself. They signal a move towards a way of living where each moment is met with awareness and choice rather than avoidance and fear.

Identifying Your Triggers: What Pushes You Away?

In the labyrinth of human emotions and interactions, certain moments act like keys turning into locks, opening doors to behaviors we might not fully understand. These keys, or triggers as we often call them, can provoke patterns of behavior deeply entrenched within us, particularly when it comes to avoidant attachment. Understanding what these triggers are and how they affect you is like mapping the hidden wires of a complex circuit—it allows you to see the connections that cause certain reactions and, crucially, gives you a chance to reroute them.

Triggers for avoidant behaviors can vary widely but often revolve around feelings of vulnerability or fear that intimacy might lead to losing one's sense of self or control. It could be as straightforward as a partner asking for more time together or as subtle as a friend sharing personal challenges and expecting you to do the same. Even positive changes, such as moving in with a partner or discussing future plans, can act as triggers if they stir underlying fears of entrapment or suffocation. The first step in managing these triggers is to identify them, which requires a blend of self-reflection and observation. You might start by looking back at past relationships or interactions to pinpoint moments when you felt compelled to pull away. What were the common elements in these situations? Was there a particular phrase, action, or emotional expression that made you want to retreat? Documenting these observations can help you detect patterns and prepare for future interactions.

Once you've identified your triggers, the next step is developing a strategy for handling them. This is where creating a trigger response plan comes into play. Such a plan involves outlining proactive steps to take when you feel triggered. For instance, if discussing future plans makes you anxious, your plan might include setting boundaries about how often and in what context this topic is brought up. Alternatively, it could involve preparing calm, honest responses that communicate your feelings and needs, such as, "I value our relationship and our discussions about the future, but sometimes I feel overwhelmed. Can we approach these conversations more gradually?" The key is to create responses that respect both your boundaries and the relationship, rather than defaulting to withdrawal.

Learning from your triggers can transform them from obstacles to opportunities for growth. Each trigger has something to teach you about your fears, needs, and boundaries. By engaging with them thoughtfully, you can begin to loosen their hold on you, making room for more adaptive, healthy ways of relating to others. This learning process can also strengthen your relationships. When you understand your triggers and communicate them to others, you pave the way for deeper understanding and support from those around you. It opens up a conversation that can lead to more trust and intimacy, as it allows others to understand your reactions and respect your needs.

Integrating this knowledge and these strategies into your daily life enhances your ability to navigate complex emotional landscapes with greater ease and confidence. It empowers you to take control of your reactions by understanding their origins and plotting a new course whenever you encounter them. This proactive approach not only diminishes the power of triggers over time but also enriches your relationships, making them more resilient and fulfilling. As you continue to explore and address these triggers, remember that each insight gained is a step toward a more connected and authentic life, one where relationships are experienced as sources of joy rather than anxiety.

The Power of Pause: Reflecting Before Retreating

In the ebb and flow of daily interactions and emotions, there exists a moment—often fleeting—where the choice hangs in the balance between engagement and retreat. For those accustomed to an avoidant attachment style, the default in these moments might lean towards withdrawal, a step back into the familiar comfort of solitude when the waters of intimacy seem threatening. Yet, within this moment lies a powerful opportunity for transformation: the pause. This pause is not a mere hesitation but a conscious decision to hold space for reflection before acting on the instinct to withdraw. It's akin to pressing a gentle but firm hand on the chest of your impulses, asking them to wait, to breathe, to consider other possibilities.

Instilling the habit of pausing is akin to developing any skill—it requires practice, patience, and persistence. Begin by identifying the scenarios in which you're most likely to retreat. Is it during a deep conversation with a friend? Or perhaps when a partner expresses the need for more closeness? Once you've pinpointed these situations, you can start to implement the pause. Next time you feel the urge to pull away, instead of acting on it, permit yourself to pause. This doesn't mean you have to engage more deeply or change the interaction course immediately; it simply means allowing yourself a moment to reflect. During this pause, take a few deep breaths to center yourself. This act of breathing deeply is not just a filler for time—it's a way to physiologically calm your nervous system and grant yourself the mental space necessary for reflection.

Reflecting during this pause involves asking yourself some key questions: What am I feeling right now? What thoughts are running through my head? Am I afraid of something? If so, what is that fear? Is my reaction of wanting to retreat in alignment with my deeper values or desires? This self-inquiry is crucial because it helps you understand the motivations behind your urge to withdraw. It shifts your perspective from a reactive stance to a more considered one, where choices can be made not out of habit but out of conscious decision-making. You might realize that the fear driving your desire to retreat is based on past experiences that aren't relevant to the current situation. Or, you might affirm that you genuinely need space, but now you can articulate this need to others clearly and calmly, rather than simply disappearing or closing down.

The benefits of developing this pause habit are manifold. Over time, pausing can help you respond to situations more thoughtfully, reducing the frequency and intensity of avoidant behaviors. It can transform your relationships, as you're better able to communicate your needs and boundaries in ways that others can understand and respect. Moreover, pausing enhances your self-awareness, as it forces you to confront and understand your feelings and reactions. This understanding is vital for personal growth, as it lays the foundation for more adaptive coping mechanisms that can replace old patterns of avoidance.

Ultimately, the power of the pause in the context of avoidant attachment is about reclaiming control over your emotional responses. It allows you to navigate your relational world not on autopilot but as an active pilot, aware of the terrain and capable of making informed decisions about how to engage with it. This skill, once honed, is not just about managing avoidant tendencies—it's about enriching your entire emotional life, opening doors to deeper connections and more fulfilling interactions that were previously obscured by the fog of haste and habit. As you continue to practice and strengthen this habit, you'll likely find that what once felt like an overwhelming urge to retreat becomes a more manageable impulse, one that you can observe, understand, and direct in ways that align with your deepest desires for connection and autonomy.

Emotional Literacy: Naming and Understanding Your Feelings

In the nuanced dance of human emotions, being able to identify and name what you feel is akin to reading a map in a foreign city—it doesn't necessarily change the landscape, but it does help you navigate it more effectively. For those with a dismissive and avoidant attachment style, developing a rich emotional vocabulary is particularly crucial. Often, emotions are experienced as vague disturbances that prompt withdrawal rather than as signals worth exploring. This can lead to a cycle where feelings, especially those that evoke vulnerability, are not fully acknowledged, influencing behaviors in ways that might not align with one's deeper desires for connection and understanding.

Expanding your emotional vocabulary involves more than just adding new words to your lexicon; it's about deepening your engagement with your own emotional states. This can start with simple exercises designed to help you differentiate between similar feelings. For example, there's a subtle difference between feeling 'irritated' and 'frustrated' or 'nervous' and 'anxious.' Each word paints a slightly different emotional landscape, and understanding these nuances can provide clearer insights into your reactions and decisions. You might begin by keeping a daily log where you describe your emotional state at different times throughout the day, using as specific terms as possible. Over time, this practice can sharpen your ability to pinpoint exactly how you're feeling, which in turn, can give you more control over your reactions.

Linking these feelings to your behaviors is the next pivotal step. It's one thing to recognize that you feel 'anxious' and another to understand how this anxiety influences your behavior, perhaps by prompting you to cancel plans or avoid discussions about your feelings. By tracking both your emotions and your actions, you can start to see patterns. Maybe you notice that you tend to withdraw when you feel criticized, or you get defensive when you're sad. These insights are invaluable because they offer you a blueprint of your emotional triggers and habitual responses, allowing you to consider alternative ways of reacting that might lead to more fulfilling interactions.

The role of emotional literacy in relationships cannot be overstated. Being fluent in the language of emotions can transform your interactions with others, allowing for deeper and more meaningful connections. When you can accurately convey how you feel, you invite others to understand your perspective more clearly. This can be particularly transformative in intimate relationships, where misunderstandings about emotional states can lead to conflict or disconnection. For instance, being able to tell your partner, "I'm feeling overwhelmed right now, and I need some time to myself," provides clarity and prevents misinterpretations that might arise if you simply withdraw without explanation.

To cultivate this skill, consider engaging in emotional expression exercises. These can be as simple as having a conversation with a close friend or therapist where you practice expressing your feelings openly and clearly. Alternatively, role-playing exercises can provide a safe space to experiment with expressing different emotions and observing how articulating your feelings can alter the course of an interaction. These exercises not only improve your ability to communicate your feelings but also help build confidence in your capacity to handle emotional exchanges, which can be particularly challenging if you're used to avoiding them.

As you become more adept at recognizing, naming, and expressing your emotions, you may find that your relationships begin to change. You might experience fewer misunderstandings and feel a greater sense of connection and intimacy. This doesn't mean that the process is always comfortable—engaging more deeply with your emotions can stir up vulnerabilities and fears. However, the rewards of such engagement are significant, offering a richer, more nuanced experience of both your inner world and your relationships. This emotional literacy is not just a tool for personal growth; it's a bridge to deeper connections with others, a way to bring more authenticity and understanding into your interactions, enhancing the quality of both your personal and professional relationships.

Chapter 5

Embracing Vulnerability for Stronger Bonds

Picture yourself standing at the edge of a high diving board for the first time. Below you, the water sparkles invitingly, but the height is dizzying, the air cool against your skin. There's a part of you that wants to jump, to experience the thrill and the splash, yet another part resists, gripped by a visceral fear of the unknown depth below. This moment, caught between a leap and a retreat, is much like the experience of embracing vulnerability when you have an avoidant attachment style. It's not just about taking the plunge but about learning to stand on that edge, to appreciate the view, and to take small, measured steps until the water below seems inviting rather than intimidating.

Small Steps Towards Trust: Gradual Exposure to Vulnerability

The journey towards embracing vulnerability often begins with small, intentional steps. For those accustomed to maintaining a fortress around their emotions, the idea of suddenly tearing down walls can feel not only daunting but downright unsafe. Instead, think of vulnerability as a muscle that needs to be conditioned gradually to gain strength. Start in environments where you feel secure and with people who have shown themselves to be trustworthy. This could be as simple as sharing a personal story from your past with a close friend or expressing a preference in a group setting. Each small act of openness is a step towards expanding your comfort zone, and just like any skill, the more you practice, the more natural it becomes.

Trust is not built overnight, especially when your natural inclination is to protect yourself from potential hurt. Building trust is a process that involves giving a little and seeing how it's handled, then giving a little more. You might begin by sharing minor inconveniences or disappointments with friends or partners, testing the waters of their support and empathy. As you receive positive reinforcements—responses that are supportive rather than dismissive—you can gradually share more significant thoughts or feelings. This method of slowly extending trust helps mitigate the overwhelming fear that can come with sudden exposures.

On this path, every step forward, no matter how small, is a victory. It's vital to recognize and celebrate these moments because they reinforce the progress you're making. Did you open up about your feelings and find the experience to be positive? Take a moment to acknowledge this triumph. Perhaps write it down in a journal or share your progress with a therapist or a supportive friend. Celebrating these wins not only bolsters your confidence but also serves as a reminder of your capability to change and grow, even in the realms that once felt impenetrable.

Creating or finding safe spaces where you can practice vulnerability is crucial. These are environments or relationships where the stakes of sharing your true self feel lower and where the repercussions of being misunderstood are minimal. Such spaces provide the perfect training ground for vulnerability. Consider support groups, therapy sessions, or close friendships that have stood the test of time. These settings often offer not only safety but also the camaraderie of shared experiences, which can make the act of opening up feel less daunting and more normalized.

As you engage in these practices, remember that the goal is not to transform into a different person overnight but to expand your ability to experience and share your world with others. Each step, each choice to be slightly more open than you were before, is a brick in the bridge you are building toward deeper, more meaningful connections. This bridge will not be built in a day, but each brick laid is integral to its structure. Embracing vulnerability is not about reckless exposure but about gradually allowing your true self to be seen and known, about moving from the diving board into the water, one small step at a time.

Revisiting Past Hurts: Healing Old Wounds

When considering the layers of your emotional armor, it's often the oldest scars that have fortified the deepest defenses. The echoes of past hurts can resonate through your behavior and relationships, manifesting as a dismissive or avoidant attachment style that keeps emotional pain at bay. To embrace vulnerability and foster genuine connections, revisiting and healing these past wounds becomes essential. This process starts with acknowledging the hurt, not dwelling on it but understanding its impact, and beginning to dismantle the walls built around your heart.

The first step in recovery is to acknowledge the pain. This might feel counterintuitive, especially if you've spent years minimizing or ignoring it. Acknowledgment doesn't mean reliving the pain but recognizing that the experiences that caused it were significant and affected you deeply. This might involve identifying events or relationships that left emotional scars—perhaps a betrayal by a close friend, neglect by a caregiver, or a harsh breakup. Reflecting on these experiences honestly allows you to see how they might be influencing your current relationships. It invites you to consider how the fears of re-experiencing such pain might be holding you back from forming closer bonds with others.

To facilitate this acknowledgment, consider writing a detailed narrative of a past hurtful event. Describe what happened, how it made you feel then, and how you think it affects you now. Writing not only helps in articulating these experiences but can also offer new perspectives on them. As you write, you might discover connections between past and present behaviors that were previously obscured by your defenses. This exercise isn't about assigning blame but about gaining clarity on the origins of your protective behaviors, which is the first step toward changing them.

Once you've acknowledged the impact of past hurts, you can engage in exercises designed to facilitate healing. One effective method is the 're-scripting' exercise, where you revisit a painful memory and imagine how it could have been handled differently. This doesn't change the past, but it can alter your emotional response to it, reducing its hold on you. For instance, if you were criticized harshly as a child, you might re-script that scenario in your mind, imagining that you received support and understanding instead. By mentally practicing these alternative responses, you can begin to internalize more supportive reactions to your current emotional needs.

Another powerful exercise is the 'empty chair' technique, often used in therapy. This involves speaking to an empty chair as if it were the person who hurt you. Express everything you wish you could have said then. This exercise can be profoundly liberating, as it allows you to express emotions that were perhaps unsafe or impossible to articulate at the time. After expressing these feelings, you can also switch chairs and reply from the perspective of the other person. This can lead to insights about the situation from a different angle, potentially fostering understanding and forgiveness.

Seeking or creating closure from unresolved past experiences is crucial for healing. Closure means finding a way to feel that a painful chapter in your life has ended, allowing you to move forward without it continually impacting your present. Sometimes, closure might involve direct communication with someone from your past, but this isn't always possible or advisable. Instead, closure can be achieved symbolically. For example, you might write a letter to the person who hurt you, expressing all your thoughts and feelings. You don't have to send the letter; the act of writing it can be enough to help you feel that you've said what needed to be said.

Alternatively, a ritual like planting a tree or releasing a balloon with your written hurts attached can symbolize letting go of the pain. These acts aren't about denying what happened but about affirming your decision not to let the past control your future. They mark a commitment to moving forward, equipped with the lessons learned but no longer burdened by the emotional weight.

Forgiveness, both of others and yourself is often a pivotal part of healing from past hurts. Forgiving doesn't mean condoning what happened. Instead, it's about freeing yourself from the burden of ongoing anger and resentment. It's a gift you give yourself, a release from the toxic ties that bind you to the past. Begin this process by reflecting on what holding onto the hurt has cost you and what might be gained by letting it go.

Self-forgiveness is equally important. You might need to forgive yourself for how you handled the situation or for the ways you've closed yourself off in response. Recognize that you did the best you could at the time with the resources and knowledge you had. Forgiving yourself is a reaffirmation of your worth and a crucial step toward opening up to others.

Finally, building emotional resilience is key to preventing old patterns from resurfacing. Resilience means building the ability to cope with difficulties and bounce back from setbacks. Strengthening resilience involves nurturing a positive self-image, maintaining a hopeful outlook, and fostering adaptable coping strategies. Cultivate resilience by engaging in activities that boost your confidence and sense of accomplishment, maintaining supportive relationships, and practicing stress-reduction techniques such as mindfulness or yoga.

Each step in this process of revisiting and healing past hurts is about gradually replacing the protective barriers of avoidance with the adaptive shields of resilience, understanding, and openness. As you work through these steps, you're not just healing old wounds; you're setting the stage for healthier, more fulfilling relationships that honor both your need for closeness and your independence. This path isn't easy, but each step brings you closer to a life where your past no longer defines your capacity for connection and where new possibilities for intimacy and trust await.

Vulnerability in Action: Practical Exercises for Everyday Life

Incorporating vulnerability into your daily life can seem like a daunting task, especially when your natural inclination may be to shield yourself from potential emotional risks. However, embracing small moments of vulnerability can lead to significant growth in your relationships and personal well-being. Think of these moments as opportunities to experiment with openness in a controlled, manageable way, allowing you to gauge and learn from each experience without feeling overwhelmed.

One practical exercise to start with involves choosing low-stakes situations where the emotional risk feels manageable. For instance, you might share an opinion in a group discussion that you would normally keep to yourself. Alternatively, consider expressing appreciation to a colleague or friend for something specific they've done. These actions might seem minor, but they require you to expose a bit of your true self. The key here is frequency rather than intensity. By regularly integrating such small acts of vulnerability into your routine, you gradually reduce the discomfort associated with opening up, paving the way for more significant disclosures in more personal relationships.

Another exercise is to engage in activities that inherently involve vulnerability, such as creative arts. Signing up for a dance class, joining a writing group, or attending a painting workshop not only places you in a new, potentially uncomfortable situation but also encourages self-expression in a supportive environment. These activities can be particularly therapeutic as they often focus more on the process of expression than on the outcome, helping you to shift focus from performance to enjoyment, from judgment to participation.

To further integrate vulnerability into your life, it's crucial to develop the ability to assess risks realistically. This involves distinguishing between actual and perceived risks of opening up. Start by asking yourself what the exact consequences of a particularly vulnerable action could be. For example, if you express a need or a preference to someone close to you, what are you really risking? Is the fear of their disappointment or judgment based on past experiences with them, or is it a general fear rooted in your avoidant tendencies?

Practicing this kind of assessment can help recalibrate your responses to situations, reducing the likelihood of automatically resorting to self-protective withdrawal. It's about questioning the narrative that vulnerability is inherently risky and recognizing that the actual outcomes are often less catastrophic than imagined. This approach not only reduces the anxiety associated with vulnerability but also enhances your decision-making process about when and how much to open up.

Establishing a feedback loop with trusted individuals can significantly enhance your vulnerability practice. This involves having open discussions with close friends or family about your attempts at vulnerability and asking for their honest feedback on how you come across and how your actions affect your relationships. This process serves two purposes: it provides you with external perspectives on your behaviors, which can be incredibly insightful, and it deepens your relationships through genuine, reciprocal engagement.

You might set up regular check-ins with a trusted friend during which you both discuss recent experiences in which you felt vulnerable. These conversations can offer support, encouragement, and sometimes a gentle push to stretch your comfort zone further. They also make the practice of vulnerability a shared journey rather than a solitary challenge, which can make the process feel more secure and integrated into your social life.

Finally, every act of vulnerability, whether it results in positive feedback or not, is a learning opportunity. It's important to reflect on each experience, considering what went well and what didn't, and what you might do differently next time. This reflection turns each instance of vulnerability into a stepping stone towards greater emotional agility and resilience.

For example, if sharing a personal story with a new acquaintance doesn't go as well as you hoped, rather than retreating into your shell, consider what might have influenced the interaction. Was it the timing, the setting, or perhaps the nature of the story itself? Was the other person's response truly negative, or could it be your interpretation that needs adjusting? Thinking about these questions can help you adjust your approach to future interactions, gradually building your confidence and skill in navigating vulnerability.

By regularly engaging in these exercises and reflections, you transform the act of vulnerability from a feared enemy to a familiar, even friendly presence in your life. Each step forward enriches your interactions and deepens your connections, illuminating the path to a more open, connected, and fulfilling life.

Setting Boundaries: Vulnerability Without Overexposure

Understanding and setting boundaries is crucial when navigating the delicate balance of sharing yourself with others while safeguarding your emotional well-being. It's about knowing where your invisible lines are drawn, not just to protect yourself from potential harm but to create a space where genuine connections can flourish without the fear of losing your sense of self. For someone with an avoidant attachment style, the act of setting boundaries is not about erecting barriers against intimacy but about delineating a clear space where intimacy can occur on your terms, at your comfort level.

Boundaries serve as guidelines that a person creates to categorize reasonable and safe ways for people to behave towards them and how they will be responded to if someone steps outside those limits. They are essential in all relationships, from the most casual acquaintances to the closest family members and partners. In your case, setting boundaries might be particularly challenging, as it involves not just identifying your comfort levels but also communicating them to others—something that might feel inherently vulnerable.

To begin setting boundaries, start with self-reflection. Identify what aspects of interactions make you feel uncomfortable or overwhelmed. Is it the frequency of contact, the type of information shared, or the expectations of emotional support? Once you have a clearer understanding of your limits, you can start to express these to others. For instance, if you're uncomfortable with spontaneous calls or visits, you might request that people text first to check if it's a good time. If deep emotional conversations drain you, you might set a boundary by specifying times when you are more open to such discussions or by asking friends to respect your need for lighter interactions at other times.

Communicating these boundaries clearly and assertively is key. Use "I" statements to communicate your needs without blaming or criticizing the other person. For example, say, "I feel overwhelmed when we talk every day. Can we check in a couple of times a week instead?" This approach respects both your needs and the other person's, reducing the likelihood of defensiveness or misunderstanding. It's important to be consistent and firm about your boundaries once they are set. This consistency helps others understand your needs and shows that you are serious about respecting your own emotional space.

Navigating pushback is part of learning to set boundaries. Keep in mind that not everyone will understand or respect your boundaries at first, especially if they are used to different dynamics with you. Some might react negatively or feel rejected. It's essential to stay firm and compassionate, reinforcing your boundaries while reassuring the person that setting these limits does not diminish your care for them. For example, if someone continues to disregard your request for advance texting before calling, you might need to remind them of your boundary and perhaps not answer unscheduled calls to reinforce your message.

Seeing boundaries as a form of strength and self-care is crucial. They are not a rejection of others but an affirmation of yourself. Firm boundaries actually foster stronger, more honest relationships because they reduce resentment and misunderstanding. They allow you to engage with others authentically and without overextending yourself, which can lead to burnout and withdrawal. In this light, boundaries are not barriers but bridges—structures that support healthy, balanced relationships where both parties feel respected and valued.

As you practice setting and maintaining these boundaries, you'll likely find that not only do your relationships improve, but your own sense of self-respect and self-worth strengthens. This growth enhances your ability to engage in relationships without fear of losing yourself, transforming vulnerability from a threat to an opportunity for connection. As you continue to work through these interactions, remember that each conversation, each boundary set, and each respectful engagement is a step towards a more balanced, fulfilling relational life where your needs and the needs of others can coexist in respectful harmony.

The Role of Self-Compassion in Embracing Vulnerability

When you encounter the raw edges of vulnerability, the instinct might be to criticize yourself for any perceived weakness or to harden against the discomfort with an internal barrage of self-judgment. This response, while understandable, can reinforce the walls you've built against intimacy and connection. In contrast, nurturing self-compassion offers a soothing balm that can transform how you engage with your own vulnerabilities, providing a safe emotional backdrop against which you can explore your feelings without fear of self-reproach.

Self-compassion is about treating yourself with the same kindness, concern, and support you would give to a close friend when they are suffering. It recognizes that being imperfect, making mistakes, and encountering life difficulties are inevitable human experiences. This mindset can be mighty when dealing with feelings of vulnerability, which often expose you to inner fears and perceived inadequacies. By adopting a stance of self-compassion, you permit yourself to be imperfect and view these moments as opportunities for growth rather than occasions for harsh self-criticism.

To cultivate self-compassion, particularly in moments when you confront your vulnerabilities, you can practice specific exercises that reinforce this mindset. One effective practice is the Self-Compassion Break, developed by Dr. Kristin Neff, a leading expert in the field. This exercise involves three main steps. First, acknowledge and label your feelings at the moment—say, "This is a moment of suffering" or "This is really hard right now." This recognition is an exercise in mindfulness, which grounds you in the reality of your experience. Second, express the universality of suffering—remind yourself that you're not alone in feeling this way, that all people have these moments of discomfort. You might say, "Suffering is a part of life," or "Others feel this way too." Finally, direct kindness towards yourself. Put your hands over your heart, feel the warmth of your palms, and say something compassionate towards yourself, like "May I give myself the compassion that I need" or "May I learn to accept myself as I am."

This practice can be particularly transformative when you face fears of rejection or judgment. It encourages a nurturing inner dialogue that counters the critical voices that often accompany attempts at vulnerability. Over time, as this compassionate self-talk becomes more habitual, you may find that the fear of opening up begins to lessen. The warmth and understanding you cultivate within yourself can radiate outward, affecting how you interact with others and fostering deeper connections.

Another crucial aspect of developing self-compassion is learning to overcome the harsh self-criticism that can be a common response among those with avoidant attachment styles. This criticism often serves as a protective mechanism, aiming to shield you from the shame or embarrassment of being seen as inadequate. However, this protection comes at a high cost, reinforcing avoidance behaviors and keeping you locked in a cycle of disconnection. To counter this, begin by observing your critical inner voice. Notice when it arises and what messages it's sending. Then, challenge these messages with evidence of your worth, your strengths, and your right to be treated with kindness, regardless of imperfections.

Self-compassion can also serve as a powerful buffer against the fear of vulnerability. By reassuring yourself that you will be kind and supportive towards your experiences and feelings, regardless of the outcome, you reduce the perceived risks associated with opening up. This security can make it easier to take small steps towards greater openness, secure in the knowledge that you will treat yourself with compassion, no matter how others respond. It's about creating an internal sanctuary that remains safe and supportive, even when external circumstances are challenging.

As you integrate these practices into your daily life, you might find that your capacity for vulnerability increases. With each act of self-compassion, you are effectively rewiring your response to fear and discomfort, replacing criticism and avoidance with kindness and acceptance. This shift not only enhances your relationships but also deeply enriches your internal world, creating a landscape where growth and healing can flourish amidst the challenges of human connection.

Remember, the act of opening up is not just about revealing your past; it's about enriching your present relationships and embracing a future where you are seen and understood more fully. As you move forward, carry with you the understanding that sharing your story is a selective process that involves thoughtful timing, choosing the right audience, and crafting your narrative in a way that feels true to you. This process is an integral part of your larger path towards deeper emotional connections and self-acceptance.

Chapter 6
Shadow Work and Inner Healing

I magine you're walking through a dimly lit hallway, pictures hanging obscured in the shadows. You've passed by these images every day, yet their details remain unseen, tucked away from the light. What if these images held keys to understanding the deeper parts of yourself, parts that you've kept in the dark, not out of disdain but perhaps out of fear or unawareness? This exploration is akin to shadow work, a profound journey into the hidden recesses of your psyche that can illuminate and transform your understanding of yourself, particularly in how you relate to others and manage your emotions.

Introduction to Shadow Work for Avoidants

Shadow work is a concept derived from the psychology of Carl Jung, which involves engaging with the 'shadow' self, those parts of our personality we often deny or ignore. For people with an avoidant attachment style, these shadows might include vulnerabilities, fears of intimacy, or desires for closeness that feels threatening to your conscious self. Engaging in shadow work means bringing light to these areas, not to eradicate them but to understand, integrate, and make peace with them. It's about turning towards the parts of yourself that you may have been taught to hide or that you feel aren't acceptable. This process is crucial because these ignored or suppressed parts can drive your behaviors in ways you might not consciously realize, particularly in how you form and maintain relationships.

For those with an avoidant attachment style, shadow work can be particularly transformative. It offers a pathway to uncover the roots of your avoidance—why closeness feels dangerous and why solitude feels safe. It can reveal the protective mechanisms that no longer serve you well and can guide you in finding healthier ways to meet your emotional needs. Engaging with your shadow can lead to greater authenticity in your relationships and a more compassionate understanding of yourself. It can decrease the internal conflict between your desire for independence and your deeper yearnings for connection, helping to harmonize your internal drives with your external behaviors.

Beginning shadow work can feel daunting; it's a journey into uncharted territories of your own psyche. Start with small, manageable steps. Journaling can be a powerful tool here. Try putting aside a few minutes each day to write about experiences or emotions that you usually avoid or dismiss. Ask yourself questions like, "What am I avoiding in this relationship?" or "What feelings am I trying to ignore?" Meditation can also be a supportive practice, offering the quiet and space needed to reflect on these deeper questions. Guided meditations focused on self-discovery can be particularly beneficial, helping you to gently confront and comfort those parts of yourself that you've been neglecting.

Creating a safe emotional environment for shadow work is essential. This work can stir up intense emotions and memories, so it's vital to ensure you feel secure and grounded. This might involve setting clear boundaries around your shadow work practices, such as limiting the time you spend on this work each day to prevent being overwhelmed. It's also wise to have support systems in place. This could be a trusted therapist experienced in Depth psychology, supportive friends or family members, or a community or group focused on personal growth. Knowing when to seek professional help is important, especially if your explorations unearth deep-seated traumas or if you find the process too challenging to manage alone. A professional can offer guidance, support, and strategies to navigate and integrate the insights you discover safely.

As you venture into the darkened corridors of your shadow self, remember that each step illuminates not just your hidden fears but also your profound capacities for change. Each piece of your shadow you integrate adds to the completeness of who you are, turning your once dimly lit path into a journey marked by greater clarity and understanding. This process, while sometimes challenging, is one of the most authentic paths to personal liberation and relational fulfillment.

Unearthing Hidden Fears: The Shadow of Independence

When you think about your independence, it might feel like a sanctuary, a place where you can be unapologetically yourself without the risk of being let down or getting too close. Yet, beneath this prized independence, there might lurk hidden fears—fears about what it truly means to depend on someone else or to be depended upon. Uncovering these fears is not about diminishing your independence but about understanding its roots and the role it plays in your life. It's about recognizing that sometimes, what we hold onto most tightly is what we fear losing the most.

Identifying these hidden fears begins with introspection. You might start by considering times when you felt the urge to pull away from someone who was getting close. What was going through your mind at that moment? Perhaps you worried they would see a part of you that you're not proud of, or maybe you feared that their needs would start to overshadow your own. Or, consider your reactions to past dependencies, whether they were relationships where you felt relied upon or situations where you had to rely on others. How did these experiences make you feel? Threatened? Trapped? Vulnerable? These emotions can be indicators of underlying fears that shape your relationship with independence.

Once these fears are brought into the light, the next step is confronting them. This confrontation is not a battle but a dialogue. It involves asking yourself why these fears are present and what they are protecting you from. For instance, if you fear dependency because it feels like a loss of control, question where this need for control comes from. Was there a time in your life when being dependent led to pain or disappointment? Understanding the origins of your fears can lessen their power, making them less likely to dictate your actions unconsciously.

Balancing independence and intimacy involves acknowledging that both are valid needs and that one does not have to exclude the other. It's about finding ways to maintain your autonomy while also allowing for closeness in your relationships. This balance might look like setting aside time for yourself to pursue your interests and recharge while also scheduling regular times to connect deeply with loved ones. It could involve being clear about your boundaries and needs, communicating openly when something doesn't feel right, and being willing to negotiate so that both your need for space and your partner's need for closeness are respected.

Personal stories from individuals who have navigated this balance can be incredibly illuminating. Consider the story of Alex, who identified as having a dismissive avoidant attachment style. Alex loved his independence and saw it as integral to who he was. Yet, in his mid-thirties, he found himself feeling isolated and unfulfilled in his relationships. Through therapy, Alex began to explore his fear that relying on others would inevitably lead to disappointment, a belief rooted in early experiences of being let down by his caregivers. By acknowledging and processing these past hurts, Alex gradually learned to open up to his partner about his needs and fears. He found that this vulnerability did not lead to the loss of independence he feared but instead to a deeper, more satisfying connection.

Engaging in this kind of shadow work involves patience and courage. It requires you to examine and challenge deeply held beliefs about what it means to be independent and what it means to be close to someone. The process can stir up discomfort and even pain, but it also holds the promise of leading to greater self-understanding and more fulfilling relationships. As you continue this exploration, remember that the goal is not to discard your independence but to understand it more fully. This understanding can empower you to form connections that honor your need for autonomy while also embracing the richness of intimacy.

Re-parenting Yourself: Healing Childhood Wounds

The concept of re-parenting is a transformative approach to self-healing that involves nurturing your inner child, particularly if that child experienced emotional neglect or rejection. This process is about giving yourself the care, affirmation, and emotional security you might not have received during your formative years. For those with a dismissive and avoidant attachment style, re-parenting offers a pathway to address and heal the roots of these attachment behaviors, providing a foundation for forming healthier relationships and interactions.

Re-parenting yourself is essentially an act of filling in the gaps left by your childhood experiences. It involves recognizing and addressing the unmet needs and providing for them in the here and now. This might mean offering yourself the compassion, presence, and validation you needed but did not receive. The process begins by identifying the aspects of your childhood that may have contributed to your avoidant attachment style. This could involve reflecting on moments of emotional neglect—times when your caregivers may have dismissed your feelings or needs, leaving you to fend for yourself emotionally. Recognizing these patterns is the first step to understanding how they might be influencing your current behaviors and relationships.

Once you've identified these childhood experiences, the next step is to actively provide what was missing. This can be done through various self-nurturing activities that affirm your worth and validate your emotions. For example, you might engage in dialogues with your inner child through journaling, where you express understanding and support for what you went through. You might also create affirmations that counteract the negative messages you received or internalized as a child, such as "I am worthy of love" or "My feelings are important." These affirmations serve to rewire the negative beliefs about yourself that were formed in response to early experiences.

Another powerful aspect of re-parenting involves setting boundaries that protect your inner child. This means learning to say no to situations or demands that mimic the neglect or rejection you experienced, and that trigger your avoidant tendencies. By doing so, you are not only looking after your emotional well-being but also teaching yourself that you have the agency to protect and care for your needs. This practice can significantly impact your relationships, as it encourages a more balanced approach to intimacy and independence, where you can engage without losing your sense of self or overriding your comfort levels.

The successes of those who have engaged in self-parenting often serve as powerful testimonials to the efficacy of this approach. Take, for example, the story of Maya, who grew up in a household where showing emotions was discouraged and often mocked. As an adult, Maya found herself dismissing her own emotional needs and struggling to form close relationships. Through re-parenting, she began to consciously address her emotional needs, allowing herself the space to feel and express emotions without judgment. She set boundaries around her time and emotional energy, choosing to engage in relationships that respected and honored her needs. Over time, Maya noticed a significant shift in her self-esteem and attachment style, moving towards more secure attachments where she could be both independent and intimately connected.

In your own journey of re-parenting, remember that this process is about honoring and caring for all parts of yourself—past and present. It's about building a nurturing relationship with yourself, one that can change the narrative of your past and profoundly influence your present and future relationships. As you engage in this healing work, you'll likely find that the compassion and acceptance you cultivate for yourself extend outward, enhancing your interactions with others and allowing you to engage with more openness and less fear.

Integrating the Shadow for Wholeness and Connection

Engaging in shadow work is akin to lighting a lamp in the darker corners of your consciousness, revealing aspects of your personality that have been hidden, perhaps out of fear or discomfort. This process, while challenging, holds the potential to transform your understanding of yourself, leading to a more integrated sense of identity and healthier relationships. Embracing your full self, including the shadow aspects, is not about uncovering flaws but about acknowledging all parts of your being, thus fostering a holistic growth that permeates every facet of your life.

The integration of your shadow self is a delicate process that can significantly enhance your emotional and relational well-being. It involves recognizing and accepting those parts of yourself that you might have previously ignored or suppressed—perhaps your vulnerabilities, fears, or unmet desires. This recognition is the first step toward wholeness, a state where you no longer feel the need to segment yourself depending on whom you're with or the situation you're in. In practical terms, this might mean acknowledging that your need for independence can coexist with your deep-seated desire for intimacy and that both are valid and do not have to be in conflict. As these fragmented parts of your personality begin to merge, you may find your relationships improving as you're able to interact with others more authentically without the subconscious fear that intimacy will obliterate your independence.

Several techniques can facilitate the integration of your shadow self. One effective method is the use of reflective journaling, where you not only explore your shadow aspects but also dialogue with them. For instance, you might write a letter from the perspective of your independence, explaining why it feels threatened by closeness. Then, you could write a response from the perspective of your desire for intimacy, discussing its needs and how it feels neglected. This exercise can help create an internal dialogue that acknowledges and respects all parts of yourself, reducing internal conflict and fostering a more harmonious internal environment.

Another powerful integration technique involves visualization exercises where you imagine a meeting between your conscious self and your shadow self. In this visualization, you can create a safe, neutral space where both sides can express their fears and desires without judgment. The key is to approach this meeting with an attitude of openness and curiosity rather than criticism. This technique helps not only recognize and accept your shadow aspects but also understand their needs and how these can be met in healthy, constructive ways.

Professional guidance can be invaluable in working through the complexities of shadow work, especially during the integration process. A therapist trained in Depth psychology or a similar approach can provide the support and framework necessary for safely exploring and integrating your shadow. They can help you identify shadow aspects, understand their origins, and develop strategies for integration that respect your unique psychological landscape. This professional support is particularly crucial if the shadow work stirs up intense emotions or unresolved trauma, ensuring that the integration process promotes healing rather than inadvertently causing harm.

Success stories of shadow integration often serve as powerful testaments to the potential of this work. Consider the experience of someone who discovered that their dismissive attitude towards relationships was a defense mechanism against the fear of rejection—a shadow aspect rooted in early parental neglect. Through conscious integration work, including therapy and mindfulness practices, they were able to acknowledge this fear, understand its origins, and gradually learn to form relationships where openness and vulnerability were not only safe but welcomed. The result was not just improved relationships but a more profound sense of inner peace and wholeness, a true testament to the transformative power of embracing and integrating the shadow self.

As this exploration of shadow work concludes, remember that integrating your shadow is not about eradicating parts of yourself but about understanding and embracing them. This process enriches your sense of self, enhances your relationships, and contributes to a more authentic, fulfilled life. As you move forward, carry with you the understanding that every part of you has a role to play in your overall well-being and that acknowledging and integrating these parts can lead to profound personal and relational growth. The journey into the next chapter continues with this holistic approach, aiming to deepen your connections and enhance your emotional resilience, paving the way for a life marked by authenticity and satisfaction.

Chapter 7

Practical Strategies to Heal The Gap

Visualize yourself standing before a vast library of books, each volume representing a story you've told yourself about who you are, how you relate to others, and what you deserve in life. Some of these books are old, their pages worn from frequent revisitation, narrating tales of self-doubt and relational withdrawal. These are the stories that often resonate with a dismissive and avoidant attachment style—stories that can dictate the course of your relationships and self-esteem. But what if you could write new books? What if you could author narratives that champion your capacity for change and connection? This idea forms the cornerstone of this chapter, focusing on rewriting the narratives you live by and integrating practices that reinforce a healthier self-perception.

Rewriting the Narrative: Positive Affirmations for the Avoidant

Identifying Negative Narratives

Your journey starts with identifying the negative narratives deeply ingrained in your psyche. These narratives might sound like, "I am better off alone," or "If I get too close, I'll just get hurt." These stories often originate from past experiences where independence equated to safety and emotional closeness led to discomfort or pain. Recognizing these narratives is pivotal because they shape how you perceive and react to intimacy and relationships. Start by reflecting on your relational history and the feelings these interactions evoke. Journaling about when you feel most compelled to withdraw or shut down can illuminate patterns in your thoughts that might be contributing to your avoidant behavior. For instance, you might notice that you feel anxious and start pulling away when someone expresses a desire for more closeness. This reaction is a clue to the narrative that intimacy is threatening, a story that needs rewriting for you to form healthier relationships.

Crafting Positive Affirmations

Once you've identified the negative narratives that dominate your relational outlook, the transformative task of crafting positive affirmations begins. Affirmations are potent tools for reshaping thoughts; they are concise, positive statements that are designed to counteract deeply held negative beliefs. For example, if your narrative is "Relationships always lead to disappointment," you might develop an affirmation like, "I am capable of building fulfilling and stable relationships." The key is to formulate affirmations that resonate personally and evoke a sense of empowerment. Write these affirmations down, and make them specific and believable. The more they reflect your actual desires and values, the more impactful they will be.

Integrating Affirmations into Daily Life

To turn these affirmations from words into beliefs, integrate them into your daily routine. This integration can be as simple as repeating them aloud every morning, posting them on sticky notes around your living space, or setting reminders on your phone to revisit them throughout the day. Another effective method is to incorporate them into a mindfulness practice or meditation, where you can focus entirely on their meaning and implications without distraction. Over time, these repeated positive statements can start to overwrite the old narratives, gradually altering your subconscious beliefs about yourself and your capacity for close relationships.

Monitoring Progress

As with any personal development effort, monitoring your progress is essential to understanding how effectively these affirmations are influencing your thoughts and behaviors. Keep a journal documenting any changes you notice in your feelings towards relationships and yourself. Are you feeling more open to intimacy? Do you see a decrease in the anxiety that typically accompanies closeness? Reflecting on these questions can help you gauge the impact of your affirmations and adjust them as needed to suit your evolving outlook better. This reflective practice not only reinforces the new narratives but also empowers you to continue this journey of change, providing tangible proof of your inner growth.

This transformation through positive affirmations is not about denying your past experiences or the validity of your initial protective reactions. Instead, it's about recognizing that those experiences do not bind you and that you have the power to author a new story for yourself—one where intimacy isn't a threat but a welcome part of a balanced and fulfilling life. As you continue to engage with these new narratives, you gradually dismantle the old frameworks of fear and avoidance, paving the way for richer, more connected relationships that previously seemed unattainable.

The Role of Therapy: Finding the Right Help

In the landscape of personal growth, especially when navigating the complexities of avoidant attachment, therapy can serve as a guiding light. It will give you a structured environment where you can explore and understand the underpinnings of your behaviors and emotions with professional support. Various therapeutic approaches cater specifically to the nuances of attachment issues, each providing unique tools and insights that can aid in your emotional development.

Exploring Therapy Options

For someone dealing with avoidant attachment, cognitive-behavioral therapy (CBT) and schema therapy are particularly beneficial. CBT helps in identifying and changing cognitive distortions and behaviors that contribute to your avoidant patterns. It focuses on the 'here and now'—helping you deal with current situations and anxieties more effectively. Schema therapy, on the other hand, delves deeper into the origins of your attachment style. It explores early life experiences that have led to long-standing patterns, helping to change these schemas or broad pervasive themes to foster healthier relationships. Both therapies provide structured approaches to understanding and modifying the thoughts and behaviors that sustain avoidant attachment. Still, the choice between them can depend on whether you're more comfortable addressing present behaviors or exploring deep-rooted personal narratives.

Finding the Right Therapist

Selecting a therapist who is experienced in dealing with avoidant attachment issues is crucial. This professional should not only be well-versed in the theories and practices of relevant therapeutic approaches but also should be someone you feel comfortable with—a therapist who respects your boundaries and understands the challenges unique to your attachment style. Start by looking for therapists who specialize in attachment issues or who use CBT or schema therapy in their practice. Many therapists offer a preliminary consultation, which can be a valuable opportunity to assess how comfortable you feel with them and to ask about their experience and approach to avoidant attachment. Remember, the therapeutic relationship is a cornerstone of effective therapy, so feeling understood and safe with your therapist is paramount.

Making the Most of Therapy

Preparation can be key to optimizing your therapy sessions. Think about keeping a journal for your thoughts and relationship patterns that you can bring to your sessions. This can help provide concrete examples of your avoidant behaviors and triggers, making the sessions more focused and productive. Be open to homework or exercises that your therapist might suggest. These tasks are designed to challenge your usual patterns and encourage new learning, which is essential for making tangible changes in your attachment style. Moreover, be patient with the process. Therapy is not a quick solution but a gradual journey towards deeper self-awareness and change. The insights and transformations unfold over time, with consistent effort both within and outside the therapy sessions.

Alternative Support

If therapy seems like a big step right now, or if you're looking for additional support resources, there are alternatives that can also provide substantial help. Support groups offer a community of people who also have challenges with their avoidant attachment. These groups give you a platform to share experiences and coping strategies, reducing the isolation that often comes with this attachment style.

Online forums and workshops focused on attachment issues can give you insight and techniques that can be beneficial in understanding and managing your attachment style. These resources, while not a substitute for professional therapy, can complement your efforts to change your attachment patterns and can be especially helpful in building a support network that encourages and validates your journey toward healthier relationships.

Navigating the world of therapy and alternative support options is a significant step towards understanding and modifying the patterns underlying your avoidant attachment. Whether through engaging with a skilled therapist or participating in support groups, the resources you choose can provide you with important tools and insights, enhancing your ability to engage in more fulfilling and less fearful relationships. As you continue to explore these options, remember that each step you take is part of a broader commitment to your emotional well-being and relational health. This commitment is both courageous and rewarding.

Communicating Needs: Scripts and Strategies

Clear communication is the linchpin in expressing what you truly need and desire from your relationships. For someone with a dismissive and avoidant attachment style, this clarity in communication can sometimes feel like navigating a minefield—balancing the fear of closeness with the inherent human need for connection. The significance of articulating your needs cannot be overstated; it is crucial not only for the health of your relationships but also for your personal growth and emotional well-being. Often, the hesitation to express needs stems from a fear of vulnerability or a belief that such expressions could lead to conflict or rejection. However, redefining this narrative to view clear communication as an act of self-respect can transform your interactions, paving the way for more authentic and satisfying connections.

Developing communication scripts is an effective strategy to enhance your ability to express your needs. These scripts serve as pre-planned guidelines that can help you navigate conversations where you need to articulate your boundaries, desires, or discomforts. The key to these scripts is that they should feel authentic; they should resonate with your voice and reflect your true feelings. For instance, if you find it challenging to turn down requests that infringe on your personal time, a script might look like this: "I appreciate your thinking of me for this project, but I need to honor my existing commitments and the personal time I've set aside for myself. Can we find another way to work this out?" This script asserts your needs respectfully and opens the door for a collaborative solution, reducing the likelihood of resentment on both sides.

Practicing these scripts can further ease the discomfort that might come with new patterns of communication. Role-play exercises can be particularly beneficial. You might enlist a trusted friend or partner to practice these scenarios. The practice environment should be supportive, allowing you to experiment with different ways of saying things while receiving feedback in real time. These rehearsals can boost your confidence and help you refine your approach before taking it into more challenging real-world interactions. For example, you could role-play a situation where you need to express your need for more space in a relationship. The feedback you receive might help you fine-tune your wording to ensure your message is clear and delivered without unintended implications.

Seeking feedback on your communication efforts is crucial and should be an ongoing part of your strategy. After real-life conversations where you've used your scripts, reflect on how the interaction went and consider asking the other person for their perspective. This feedback can provide insights into how your message was received and whether your communication achieved its intended effect. Open yourself to the possibility of adjusting your approach based on this feedback. Perhaps you find that your initial attempt at setting boundaries felt too rigid or distant. With this insight, you can modify your script to include more empathetic language or to acknowledge the other person's feelings better.

This dynamic process of developing, practicing, and refining your communication scripts is not about crafting perfect conversations but about enhancing your ability to express yourself clearly and respectfully. As you become more adept at using these scripts, you'll likely find that your interactions become less stressful and more productive. Clear communication fosters understanding and respect, reducing the chances of conflicts and misunderstandings that can so often distance you from others. By investing in this skill, you not only improve your relationships but also reinforce your self-esteem and personal integrity. It's about giving voice to your needs and, in doing so, honoring your worth in every interaction.

Rebuilding Trust: Steps Toward Secure Attachment

Trust is the foundation for all secure relationships. It's the glue that binds individuals together, allowing them to feel safe, secure, and valued in each other's presence. Understanding trust involves recognizing it as a multifaceted construct composed of consistency, dependability, and emotional transparency. For someone with an avoidant attachment style, where self-reliance often overshadows relational interdependence, the concept of trust can sometimes seem foreign or fraught with vulnerability. However, the reconstruction of trust is not just possible; it is a transformative process that can lead to significantly more fulfilling relationships.

The first step in rebuilding trust is to redefine what it means to you. Consider how past experiences have colored your perceptions of trust and how these might differ from the healthier, more balanced view of trust you wish to cultivate. Trust is not just about expecting others not to hurt you but also about believing in your ability to handle situations when they don't go as planned. It involves trusting yourself to set boundaries and to communicate openly. This broader understanding of trust can be a liberating framework from which to start rebuilding.

Step-by-step trust-building then begins with small commitments. In practice, this means starting with low-risk situations where the cost of trust being broken is minimal. For instance, you might share a small piece of personal information with a friend or partner and observe their reaction. The key here is consistency; repeatedly engaging in small acts of trust can gradually build your confidence in others' reliability and your own resilience. Over time, these small steps create a new pattern of expectations and interactions, reinforcing the trustworthiness of those around you and your own trust in them.

Patience and consistency are crucial in this process. Building trust is not an overnight task; it requires time and repeated evidence that new behaviors and responses are sustainable. This can be particularly challenging if you're accustomed to quick judgments and retreats in relationships. Be patient with yourself and others as you navigate this new terrain. Recognize that setbacks are part of the process, not signs of failure. Each interaction provides valuable information about where trust stands and what might need more attention.

Handling setbacks effectively is central to successfully rebuilding trust. When disappointments occur, view them as opportunities for learning and growth rather than reasons to reinforce old barriers. Suppose a friend forgets an important event you shared with them, and it triggers your old fears about unreliability. Instead of withdrawing, address the issue directly. Discuss how the oversight made you feel and listen to their perspective. This open communication can clarify misunderstandings and reinforce the importance of reliability and attentiveness in your relationships. Each of these conversations can further cement the foundation of trust, showing that even when things go wrong, the relationship can withstand stress and recover.

In the continuous effort to rebuild trust, remember that each positive interaction, each fulfilled promise, and each successful communication adds a brick to the foundation of a more secure attachment. This evolving trust not only enhances your relationships but also deeply enriches your personal growth, offering a more stable, connected approach to life and love. As you engage with these steps toward secure attachment, let each small success inspire and motivate further efforts, weaving a stronger, more resilient fabric of connections that support and enrich your life in ways you might once have thought impossible.

Self-Soothing Techniques for Anxiety and Fear

Navigating through daily life, moments arise that test your balance, pulling at the threads of your calm. For you, these moments might feel particularly overwhelming due to your dismissive and avoidant attachment style, where anxiety and fear can sometimes take the wheel, driving you into habitual retreats from closeness and connection. However, developing effective self-soothing techniques can serve as an anchor, a personal toolkit that empowers you to maintain your composure and presence, especially during times of distress. These techniques are not just about temporary relief but about cultivating a deeper resilience that supports your emotional well-being and enhances your capacity for engaging in meaningful relationships.

Grounding Exercises

Grounding techniques are foundational in your toolkit for navigating anxiety and fear. These exercises are designed to divert your focus from distressing emotions or thoughts and bring your awareness to the present moment—a practice that can be both calming and centering. One effective grounding technique involves the '5-4-3-2-1' method, which engages all your senses to anchor you in the now. Start by naming five things you can see around you at the moment—

perhaps a tree swaying outside your window, a book on your desk, or a cup of coffee. Next, identify four things you can touch, like the texture of your clothing, the cool surface of your table, or the warmth of a sunbeam. Continue by acknowledging three things you can hear, which might be distant traffic, birdsong, or the hum of a computer. Then, focus on two things you can smell—maybe the lingering scent of your morning toast or a hint of perfume. Finally, recognize one thing you can taste, like a mint on your tongue or a sip of water. This exercise can significantly dial down anxiety by connecting you with your immediate environment, pulling your thoughts away from distress and into a state of mindful presence.

Sensory Engagement Techniques

Expanding on the use of your senses, sensory engagement techniques can be tailored to provide comfort and distraction from anxiety. These techniques involve intentionally engaging one or more of your senses to evoke calm and relaxation. For instance, listening to calming music can have a soothing effect on your nervous system, reducing anxiety and elevating mood. Create a playlist of music that elicits feelings of peace or nostalgia for you, and use it as a go-to resource when you feel overwhelmed. Similarly, aromatherapy involves the use of scents to affect mood and emotion positively. Essential oils like lavender, chamomile, or sandalwood can be used in a diffuser or applied to pulse points to help reduce stress and promote relaxation. The key is to experiment with different scents to discover which ones offer you the most relief and comfort, integrating them into your daily routine as a quick and accessible way to manage anxiety.

Creating a Self-Soothing Kit

To consolidate your self-soothing strategies, consider assembling a personalized kit that includes items designed to calm and comfort you during anxious moments. Your kit might include a small vial of your favorite essential oil for aromatherapy, a stress-relief ball or fidget spinner to engage your sense of touch, a pair of earplugs to listen to your calming playlist, and a set of affirmation cards that you can read to remind yourself of your strengths and capabilities. You might also include a favorite snack or herbal tea that helps soothe you. Keep this kit in a place where you can easily access it, perhaps in your bag or at your desk, ensuring that you have these tools at hand whenever anxiety arises. This kit not only serves as a practical resource for managing stress but also as a symbolic reminder that you have the power to regulate your emotions and maintain your serenity, even in challenging moments.

Through these self-soothing techniques—grounding exercises, sensory engagement, positive affirmations, and a personalized soothing kit—you equip yourself with a versatile set of tools that enhance your ability to manage anxiety and fear effectively. These practices empower you to remain present and engaged in your life, supporting your journey toward more secure attachments and fulfilling relationships. As you continue to integrate and personalize these techniques, they become more than just responses to distress; they transform into proactive strategies for cultivating a life characterized by greater emotional resilience and more profound, more meaningful connections.

Visualization for Emotional Healing and Connection

Imagine your mind as a serene, expansive landscape where each thought and memory creates its own horizon. Visualization, a powerful mental technique, allows you to sculpt this landscape deliberately, planting seeds of healing, connection, and self-discovery. Through guided imagery, you can create tranquil scenes that not only offer relaxation but also foster profound inner change. This approach harnesses your brain's ability to simulate experiences, positively influencing your emotions and behaviors without physical interaction. It's particularly useful for someone with an avoidant attachment style, as it provides a safe space to explore emotional depths and rehearse new relational scenarios without immediate real-world stakes.

Guided Imagery for Relaxation

To begin with visualization for relaxation, find a quiet space where you won't be disturbed. Close your eyes and take several deep breaths, honing in on the rise and fall of your chest to anchor your mind in the present. Now, imagine a place where you feel completely at peace. This could be a real location you've visited before, like a quiet beach at sunset, or a fictional serene setting, such as a garden filled with flowers gently swaying in a breeze. Visualize the details of this place—the colors, the sounds, and the scents. Picture yourself there, feeling the environment's calmness seep into your bones. Engage all your senses to make the experience as vivid as possible. The goal here is to create a mental refuge that you can return to whenever the outside world feels overwhelming or when your avoidance tendencies kick in. Over time, this mental practice can help reduce anxiety and improve your emotional resilience, making it easier to handle interpersonal challenges.

Visualization for Future Relationships

In addition to fostering relaxation, visualization can be a proactive tool for shaping your future relationships. Here, the focus shifts from passive relaxation to active creation. Start by envisioning yourself in a scenario where you are experiencing a healthy, connected relationship. Picture the interactions—perhaps you're sharing a laugh with a partner over coffee, or you're discussing a book with a close friend, feeling genuinely engaged and open. Visualize your body language, the expressions on your face, and the warmth between you. The key is to experience these positive interactions vividly, to feel the emotions they stir in you. This practice not only primes you to expect and cultivate such healthy dynamics but also helps rewrite internal scripts about relationships being sources of stress or hurt. By regularly imagining positive relational experiences, you reinforce the belief that such interactions are possible and desirable, gradually reshaping your expectations and behaviors towards intimacy.

Healing Past Wounds through Visualization

Visualization also offers a pathway to heal past relational wounds, which is crucial for altering avoidant attachment behaviors. In this practice, you revisit painful or unresolved experiences from your past but from a perspective of empowerment and healing. Imagine revisiting a moment when you felt rejected or misunderstood. In your visualization, alter the outcome or introduce new elements that change the scenario's emotional tone. Perhaps you envision your present self stepping into the scene, offering support or understanding to your younger self, or you imagine a different response from the other person involved—one that validates rather than dismisses your feelings. This method of reimagining past events can help to loosen their grip on your psyche, allowing you to forge a more compassionate view of your past and a more hopeful outlook for your future interactions.

Connecting with your Inner Self

Finally, visualization can facilitate a profound connection with your inner self, strengthening self-compassion and understanding—qualities that are often overshadowed by self-critical thoughts in those with avoidant attachment. Visualize meeting your inner self, perhaps in the peaceful setting you created for relaxation. See this aspect of yourself as a distinct entity sitting across from you, and engage in a dialogue. Ask questions you might avoid: "What do you fear the most in relationships?" or "What do you need to feel safe?" Listen to the responses and offer reassurance. This exercise can help you uncover deep-seated emotions and needs, fostering an internal environment of acceptance and empathy. By constantly connecting with your inner self, you enhance your self-awareness and develop a more supportive and understanding relationship with yourself, which is essential for navigating the complexities of intimacy and relationships in the external world.

Through these visualization practices—whether you're seeking relaxation, envisioning healthier relationships, healing from past wounds, or connecting with your inner self—you harness the power of your mind to support and enhance your emotional and relational growth. Each session builds on the last, deepening your understanding of yourself and expanding your capacity for emotional connection, gradually reshaping your attachment style towards one that embraces, rather than avoids, closeness.

The Art of Apology: Repairing After Retreat

In the intricate workings of relationships, missteps are bound to happen. Especially for you, where retreat might often seem like the safest response to conflict or discomfort, the moments where these retreats cause unintended hurt are particularly challenging. Recognizing when an apology is necessary and delivering it sincerely becomes a vital skill in mending and deepening the connections you might have strained or even broken in your moments of withdrawal. It's about acknowledging the impact of your actions, intentional or not, and showing a commitment to change—an essential step for anyone seeking to overcome avoidant behaviors and foster healthier relationships.

Recognizing the Need to Apologize

The first step in this process is to recognize when an apology is due. This might seem straightforward, but for someone with a dismissive and avoidant attachment style, it can be a complex realization. Often, the instinct to protect oneself from emotional exposure can overshadow the recognition of the other person's hurt. Start by reflecting on recent interactions where you've pulled back or shut down emotionally. Did your retreat leave someone feeling ignored, misunderstood, or devalued? Sometimes, it might not be obvious until you notice a change in the other person's behavior towards you—perhaps they've become colder, or they express hurt or confusion. Acknowledging these signals is your cue that an apology might be necessary to address the emotional gap your retreat has caused.

Components of a Sincere Apology

A sincere apology has several key components. First, it requires acknowledgment of the hurt caused. This means explicitly stating what you did and recognizing how it affected the other person. For example, saying, "I realize that by shutting down and not responding to your messages, I made you feel unimportant and ignored," directly addresses the behavior and its emotional impact. Next, express genuine remorse for the hurt caused, not just for the action itself. This shows that you understand and care about the emotional consequences of your actions. Lastly, a crucial part of a sincere apology involves a commitment to change. This doesn't mean promising never to retreat again—that's an unrealistic expectation for anyone, especially if you're naturally inclined to avoidant behavior. Instead, focus on realistic commitments, like, "I'm working on communicating more openly when I feel overwhelmed, rather than withdrawing."

Restorative Actions

Actions often speak louder than words, and this is particularly true in the context of apologies. Including restorative actions—that is, steps you take to make amends and demonstrate your commitment to change—can significantly enhance the effectiveness of your apology. These actions should be tailored to the situation and the person you've hurt. For instance, if you cancel plans at the last minute, a restorative action might be rescheduled at a time that's convenient for them, showing that you value their time and company. Or, if you failed to support a friend in a moment of need due to your withdrawal, offering your support in a specific, tangible way can demonstrate your sincerity. These actions not only help to heal the rifts caused by your retreat but also reinforce your verbal commitment to doing better in the future.

Receiving Apologies

As much as it's crucial to know how to apologize, understanding how to receive apologies with grace is equally important. This involves acknowledging the other person's effort to make amends and not dismissing their apology, which can discourage future openness. When someone apologizes to you, try to listen fully without interrupting or downplaying their feelings—express appreciation for their apology, which can encourage more open and honest communication moving forward. Also, permit yourself to express how the incident affected you if you feel it's necessary. This can be part of your healing process and can help the other person understand your perspective better, fostering deeper mutual understanding.

In navigating the complexities of relationships, mastering the art of apology is a powerful tool in your emotional toolkit. It not only mends bridges and heals wounds but also deepens your connections through demonstrated empathy and responsibility. As you practice these steps, you cultivate a relationship landscape where openness, responsibility, and mutual respect are the norms, paving the way for more secure and fulfilling interactions.

In conclusion, this chapter has explored various practical strategies to help you navigate the intricate aspects of relationships and personal growth. From rewriting negative narratives with positive affirmations to understanding the therapeutic journey and from engaging in behavioral experiments to mastering the art of communication and apology, each section has equipped you with tools to foster change and enhance your interactions. As we move forward, these foundational skills will support your continued journey toward developing healthier, more secure attachment styles and enriching your relationship experiences.

Chapter 8

Exercises for Couples to Move Into Secure Attachment

Building trust with your partner is like crafting a tapestry together, each thread representing a shared moment, a word, a silence, or a secret. Just as the quality of the threads and the intricacies of the weave determine the beauty and strength of the tapestry, so do the ways you communicate and connect, which shape the resilience and richness of your relationship. This chapter is dedicated to enhancing those threads, strengthening the weave through dialogue exercises that not only improve communication but deepen understanding and intimacy between you and your partner.

Dialogue Exercises to Enhance Connection

Active Listening Skills Practice

In the realm of relationships, active listening is akin to a dance where each step, each move of your partner, is met with your attentive presence and response. It's about fully engaging with your partner's words, emotions, and, most importantly, the unspoken feelings behind them. To foster this skill, you and your partner can engage in exercises designed to shift the focus from merely hearing to truly understanding each other. Begin with a simple activity where one of you shares an experience or feeling while the other purely listens, refraining from interrupting or planning a response. After sharing, the listener repeats back what they heard, capturing not just the words but the emotions conveyed. This practice not only improves your ability to listen but also makes your partner feel profoundly seen and heard, reinforcing the emotional bond between you.

Expressing Needs and Desires

For someone with an avoidant attachment style, expressing needs and desires might feel like navigating a minefield blindfolded. However, clear communication of your needs is crucial for a healthy relationship. To ease into this, start with exercises that focus on expressing everyday preferences, like choosing a movie or deciding on a meal. Gradually, it escalates to more significant matters, such as discussing your needs for personal space or connection. By practicing in low-stakes scenarios, you build the confidence and skills necessary for more critical conversations. Remember, the goal is to express your needs clearly and respectfully without the fear of overexposure or misunderstanding.

The Mirror Technique

The mirror technique is a powerful exercise for ensuring that you and your partner understand each other accurately. In this exercise, after one partner shares something important, the other mirrors back what they've heard before responding. This mirroring can clarify misunderstandings immediately and validate each person's feelings, ensuring that both partners feel understood. Moreover, it teaches you to pause and consider your partner's perspective, fostering a deeper connection and respect for each other's viewpoints.

Sharing Personal Histories

Sharing personal histories is about unveiling the narratives of your past that shape who you are today. This exercise involves each partner discussing their significant life events, family dynamics, and past relationships, not as a mere recount but as a way to reveal the emotional impacts of these experiences. By understanding each other's backgrounds, you develop a deeper empathy and appreciation for how these histories influence your current behaviors and reactions within the relationship. It's about seeing the tapestry of your partner's life and understanding the threads that contribute to the person they are in the present.

Together, these exercises weave a stronger, more intimate bond between you and your partner, turning communication into a tool for connection rather than a battleground for avoidance. Each dialogue practice opens new doors to understanding, caring, and ultimately, loving each other more deeply, allowing you to create a relationship that is not only about surviving together but thriving together.

Building Empathy: The Two-Sided Story Technique

Empathy, that profound emotional bridge that connects you to someone else's inner world, is often a challenge for those who naturally lean towards a dismissive and avoidant attachment style. It involves lowering your emotional defenses, something that might not come easily or instinctively. However, cultivating empathy is not just about understanding others; it's about enriching your relationships and providing a deeper dimension of connection that can bring immense satisfaction and stability. The Two-Sided Story Technique is a transformative exercise designed to foster this understanding by exploring issues from both partners' perspectives.

In this technique, each partner takes turns sharing their viewpoint on a particular issue, not just recounting the facts but expressing how the situation made them feel. The key here is to refrain from interjecting or defending your stance until both sides have been articulated. This practice encourages listening, not for points to argue, but to truly understand where the other is coming from. For example, suppose a disagreement arose from a misunderstood comment. In that case, one partner might explain how the comment felt dismissive and hurtful, while the other might share their original intent and feelings of frustration when the response seemed disproportionate. This open exchange can illuminate how different interpretations of the same event can lead to conflict, paving the way for greater understanding and compassion.

Empathy-building scenarios further enhance this technique by placing partners in hypothetical situations that require empathy and understanding. These scenarios are designed to be slightly challenging, pushing you outside your comfort zone to explore emotional responses that might not occur in your everyday interactions. For instance, you might imagine a situation where one partner has experienced a significant personal setback, like a job loss or a family issue. Discussing how each of you would handle the situation, both as the one affected and as the supporter, can reveal underlying expectations and emotional needs that might not surface until a real crisis occurs. This proactive approach not only builds empathy but also prepares you both for handling life's more challenging moments together.

Reflective feeling exercises are another component of this technique. After sharing perspectives, each partner reflects on the feelings and emotions they heard the other express. This reflection is not just about repeating words but about showing that the emotional content was truly heard and felt. "I hear that you felt overlooked when I went straight to my computer after dinner, and that hurt because it seemed like I prioritized work over our time together," one might say. This practice validates each partner's feelings and shows that they are a crucial aspect of the relationship dynamic, fostering a deeper emotional connection and mutual respect.

Cultivating compassion during conflicts might seem counterintuitive, especially when emotions run high. However, viewing disagreements as opportunities for growth rather than threats can transform the way you engage in conflicts. Instead of approaching a disagreement with the mindset of winning or defending your position, consider what this conflict can teach both of you. What is it about this issue that triggers such strong emotions? Is there a pattern that can be identified and perhaps altered for better outcomes? Engaging with these questions can turn a potentially divisive situation into a constructive one, where both partners feel they are working together to solve a problem, not battling against each other.

Through these practices, the Two-Sided Story Technique not only enhances empathy but also strengthens the relationship's foundation by weaving a stronger, more compassionate bond. As you continue to engage in these exercises, you may find that they not only improve your relationship but also challenge you to grow personally, becoming more attuned to the complexities of your own and others' emotional worlds.

Partner Exercises for Continuous Emotional Growth

In relationships, growth is not a destination but a continuous journey of discovery and adaptation. For you and your partner, embarking on this path requires a commitment to not only understand each other better but also to evolve together. Setting shared goals for emotional growth and connection is a profound step in this process. Imagine sitting down together, cups of coffee in hand, and discussing what you both hope to achieve in your relationship over the next year. These goals could range from improving communication to spending more quality time together or supporting each other's personal ambitions. The act of setting these goals together builds a feeling of teamwork and shared purpose, which is essential for a harmonious relationship. It's not just about agreeing on what you want to achieve, but also why these goals matter. This clarity can transform abstract aspirations into concrete plans, making it easier to work towards them collectively.

Empathy, often overshadowed by more immediate concerns in a relationship, is the glue that binds these goals. It's the ability not just to see but also to feel the world from your partner's perspective. Developing this can be particularly challenging if you tend to withdraw emotionally, yet it's crucial for deepening your connection. Consider exercises specifically designed to enhance empathy, such as 'emotional mirroring,' where you and your partner share how you felt during specific moments of your day, trying to connect not only with the narrative but also with the emotions involved. Another effective exercise is role reversal, where you both act out how you think the other would respond in a given situation. This not only adds a lighthearted element to understanding each other's perspectives but also deepens your appreciation for each other's emotional responses.

Communication challenges can often become roadblocks in achieving these goals, especially when they involve expressing vulnerabilities or addressing conflicts. Introducing communication challenges as a regular part of your interaction can turn these potential roadblocks into opportunities for strengthening your bond. Start with something simple, like discussing a movie plot, and gradually escalate to more personal topics like fears and dreams. These challenges should encourage openness and honesty, pushing both of you out of your comfort zones in a supportive and structured manner. It's not about winning an argument or proving a point but about understanding each other's thoughts and feelings more clearly. Over time, these challenges can significantly improve the way you communicate, making it easier to handle difficult conversations and reduce misunderstandings.

Finally, celebrating vulnerability within the relationship can dramatically shift how you perceive openness and emotional exposure. Create exercises that reward vulnerability, such as sharing a personal story from your past that you feel shapes who you are today, followed by a supportive discussion about it. Another exercise could involve acknowledging and discussing your fears about the relationship or personal insecurities. The key here is to create a safe space where showing vulnerability is not only accepted but celebrated. This could be as simple as expressing gratitude towards each other after sharing, or more elaborate, like planning a special date night whenever one of you takes a significant step in opening up. These celebrations act as positive reinforcements, making you both more comfortable and willing to share your inner worlds.

Through these exercises, you and your partner can build a dynamic relationship that not only withstands the test of time but also deepens in love, understanding, and respect. As you continue to engage in these practices, remember that each small step is part of a larger picture of mutual growth and happiness.

The Appreciation List: Fostering Gratitude in Relationships

In the tapestry of a relationship, threads of gratitude can add vibrant colors that enhance the overall picture, making it more resilient and beautiful. The practice of creating and sharing daily appreciation lists is a simple yet profoundly impactful way to foster a culture of gratitude within your relationship. Imagine each day taking a moment to jot down things you genuinely appreciate about your partner. This could range from acknowledging their knack for making perfect morning coffee to appreciating their patience during your moments of stress. The key here is specificity and sincerity—the more detailed your appreciation, the more valued your partner is likely to feel.

As you incorporate this practice into your daily life, consider setting a specific time each day for this activity, perhaps during breakfast or right before bed. This regularity turns gratitude from a spontaneous gesture into a consistent practice, embedding it deeply into the fabric of your relationship. Over time, this list becomes a powerful reminder of the positive aspects of your partner and the relationship, especially during moments of conflict or dissatisfaction. Sharing these lists with each other not only reinforces these positive perceptions but also opens up a space for emotional intimacy. As you express gratitude, you're also implicitly communicating that you notice and value your partner's contributions to your life, which can significantly enhance the emotional bond between you.

The foundation of gratitude transforms relationship dynamics by shifting the focus from what's lacking to what's abundant. This shift is not just about seeing the glass as half full; it's about recognizing and celebrating the water in the glass. In relationships, particularly for someone with an avoidant attachment style, it's easy to get caught up in defenses and distancing. Gratitude cuts through these defenses, fostering a positive feedback loop where kindness and appreciation lead to more of the same. Discussing the impact of this gratitude practice during moments of connection can deepen your understanding of how such positivity enhances your relationship. For instance, during a quiet evening together, you might discuss how the gratitude practice has helped you feel closer and more connected, reinforcing the practice's value and encouraging its continuation.

Gratitude is especially crucial during challenging times in a relationship. When faced with stress or conflict, it's natural to focus on the negatives, which can amplify feelings of dissatisfaction and disconnection. However, maintaining a practice of gratitude can provide a counterbalance during these periods, offering a perspective that helps preserve the bond you share even in rough waters. Encouraging each other to find and express something you're grateful for daily, even on the worst days, can be a lifeline back to connection. It's about acknowledging that, despite the current challenges, there are still aspects of your partner and relationship that you value deeply. This practice not only nurtures resilience but also serves as a constant reminder of why you are together, helping to smooth over the rough patches more quickly and effectively.

By weaving gratitude into the daily interactions of your relationship, you create a stronger, more resilient bond that can weather both the mundane and monumental challenges of life. This culture of appreciation not only enhances your current relationship dynamics but also sets a tone of mutual respect and admiration that can define your interactions for years to come. As you continue to build this practice, you may find that gratitude becomes not just something you do but a defining characteristic of how you relate to each other, transforming your relationship into a shared journey of continual appreciation and deepening connection.

Conflict Resolution Skills for a Stronger Bond

When you think of conflict, it's common to envision a battlefield—lines drawn, defenses up, each word a potential weapon. However, within the context of a relationship, conflict can be reframed as a rich soil from which deeper understanding and intimacy can grow. Think of it as a challenging workout for your relationship muscles; it's tough and might hurt at the moment, but it ultimately builds strength and resilience. Adopting this mindset allows you to approach disagreements not as threats but as opportunities for growth, where both partners can learn more about each other and find ways to harmonize their needs and desires.

One essential skill in navigating conflicts is identifying the underlying needs that fuel them. Conflicts rarely arise from the surface issues themselves, but from the unmet needs these issues symbolize. For instance, a disagreement about spending too much time at work might reflect a more profound need for appreciation or security. Unearthing these underlying needs helps you peel back the layers of your reactions during conflicts. Ask yourself or your partner questions like, "What am I really looking for in this situation?" or "What need do I feel is not being met?" This introspection can transform a conflict from a clash of opinions to a collaborative exploration of deeper desires and needs, paving the way for solutions that address the root of the problem rather than just its symptoms.

The Timeout Technique is another crucial strategy, particularly effective for those moments when emotions run high and a productive conversation seems impossible. This technique involves agreeing with your partner to take a brief break from the discussion when either of you feels overwhelmed or too emotional. The key is to treat this timeout not as an escape but as a pause for recalibration. During this pause, engage in activities that reduce your stress or help you gain a clearer perspective, such as taking a walk, meditating, or writing down your thoughts. Once both partners feel calmer and more collected, you can resume the conversation with renewed focus and decreased emotional charge, making it easier to communicate effectively and listen genuinely.

Strategies for calm discussion are the bedrock upon which constructive conflict resolution is built. Begin by setting a tone of mutual respect and openness, affirming your commitment to understanding each other's perspectives. Use "I" statements to express your feelings without blaming or criticizing your partner, such as "I feel hurt when you dismiss my ideas" instead of "You always ignore my suggestions." This approach reduces defensiveness and opens up space for empathy. Additionally, focus on being present during these discussions and actively listening without planning your rebuttal. This presence not only shows your respect for your partner's feelings but also helps you grasp the full scope of their perspective, which is crucial for finding common ground.

Finding common ground involves looking for areas where your desires and those of your partner overlap or where compromises can satisfy both parties. This search might involve some give-and-take, where you both adjust your expectations or desires to meet somewhere in the middle. For instance, if the conflict is about how to spend your leisure time together, common ground might be alternating between each partner's preferred activities each week. Emphasizing this common ground reinforces your partnership's collaborative nature, showing that despite the conflict, you both are working towards a shared goal of happiness and fulfillment.

Solution-focused conflict resolution shifts the focus from what went wrong to how to make it right. This approach involves identifying specific actions both partners can take to settle the issue and prevent similar conflicts in the future. For example, if frequent misunderstandings are the problem, one solution could be to establish a daily "check-in" ritual where you both can share your feelings and clarify any miscommunications from the day. By focusing on solutions, you foster a proactive atmosphere where challenges are met with creativity and willingness to improve, enhancing the resilience and adaptability of your relationship.

Forgiveness and reconciliation are the final pieces in the conflict resolution puzzle, sealing the cracks that conflicts might leave in your relationship's foundation. Forgiveness involves letting go of the bitterness or resentment resulting from past hurts, which is crucial for healing and moving forward. Reconciliation takes this a step further by restoring the relationship to a state of equilibrium where both partners feel valued and understood. These processes require open-hearted discussions where you both acknowledge the pain caused, express sincere apologies, and make commitments to change behaviors that hurt the other. Through forgiveness and reconciliation, you not only repair the damages of conflict but also strengthen your bond, equipping your relationship with a deeper understanding and mutual respect that can withstand future challenges.

By integrating these conflict resolution skills into your relationship dynamics, you transform potential battlegrounds into forums for fostering deeper understanding and connection. Each conflict becomes a stepping stone towards a stronger, more resilient bond characterized by mutual respect, empathy, and a commitment to collective growth. As you and your partner continue to navigate these challenges together, you build a robust foundation that supports not just enduring harmony but also a profound appreciation for each other's unique perspectives and needs.

Planning Future Dreams Together to Strengthen Bonds

Envisioning a future together is not just about setting sights on distant dreams—it's about weaving those dreams into the everyday fabric of your relationship, giving both you and your partner a shared direction and purpose. Creating a shared vision board serves as a visual and tangible manifestation of these shared dreams and goals. This activity isn't just about pasting pictures or words on a board; it's a deeply connective experience where you both get to explore and express your hopes and aspirations for the future. Start by gathering magazines, photos, quotes, or any items that resonate with your visions of the future. As you both contribute to this board, discuss why these images and words are significant to you. This process not only helps in visualizing your goals but also deepens your understanding of each other's desires and aspirations, reinforcing the bond you share.

Once your vision board is complete, it acts as a daily reminder of your goals together, inspiring both of you to work towards them actively. However, this is just the beginning. Setting specific relationship goals is the next crucial step. Facilitate a goal-setting session where you both define what you want to achieve in the short term (months) and long term (years). These goals can range from financial objectives, like saving for a home, to personal growth goals, such as committing to a weekly date night to ensure quality time together. The key here is to make these goals clear, measurable, and, importantly, agreed upon by both partners. This clarity transforms abstract dreams into actionable steps, making it easier to pursue them as a team.

Regular check-ins on these goals are essential to keep the momentum going and to make necessary adjustments. These check-ins provide an opportunity to reflect on your progress, celebrate achievements, and discuss any challenges that might be hindering your advancement. Schedule these discussions monthly or quarterly, treating them as essential appointments in your relationship calendar. During these sessions, be open about what is working and what isn't, and be willing to adapt your strategies or goals as needed. This adaptability shows that you are committed to the process of growing together, not just set on achieving static goals.

Celebrating achievements together is the most rewarding part of this process. Whether it's a small win like sticking to your date night schedule for a month or a big one like buying your first home together, take the time to celebrate these milestones. Plan special activities or outings to mark these achievements, or create a ritual that you both enjoy. These celebrations not only reinforce your bond but also remind you why you set these goals in the first place—to build a fulfilling life together.

Through these exercises—creating a vision board, setting specific goals, regular check-ins, and celebrating achievements—you and your partner can strengthen your bond by aligning your dreams and working together towards a shared future. This aligned effort not only brings you closer but also builds a foundation of mutual support and understanding that can enhance every aspect of your relationship.

As we wrap up this chapter on strengthening bonds through shared dreams and visions, remember that the essence of these exercises lies in their capability to bring you and your partner closer, turning individual dreams into a collective journey of growth and fulfillment. The practices discussed here pave the way for a deeper connection, fostering a partnership that is not only about loving in the present but also about building and dreaming together for the future. As you move forward, carry with you the understanding that every step taken together is a step towards a more connected relationship.

Chapter 9
Deepening Emotional Intimacy

Envision walking through a garden, where each path unveils a deeper shade of green, and each turn reveals a more vibrant bloom. Emotional intimacy in a relationship mirrors this garden walk, where each step taken together deepens your understanding and connection. Yet, for those with an avoidant attachment style, this path might seem obscured by a fog of apprehension and past guards. This chapter, particularly this section, is like a gentle breeze that helps clear the mist, guiding you toward being truly present in your relationships, enhancing emotional availability, and cultivating a deeper connection with those you care about.

Emotional Availability: Becoming Present in Your Relationships

Being present in a relationship means more than just being physically there; it involves opening yourself up to experiencing the moment fully with your partner, without the usual distractions or defenses. This presence is crucial, as it forms the foundation upon which deeper emotional connections are built. For someone with an avoidant attachment style, the idea of presence might trigger a reflex to retreat into your shell. However, embracing mindfulness can transform this experience, offering you tools to remain engaged without feeling overwhelmed.

Mindfulness teaches you to experience the present moment without judgment. By focusing on the here and now, you're less likely to get lost in worries about the future or regrets from the past, common triggers for avoidance. Practicing mindfulness can start with something as simple as paying attention to your breathing during a conversation, noticing when your mind wanders, and gently bringing your attention back to the interaction. This focused attention signals to your partner that you value the time and emotions being shared, fostering a closer bond.

In today's world, distractions are always at our fingertips—emails that need responding, social media notifications, and work calls that intrude upon personal time. These interruptions can be particularly detrimental to someone with an avoidant attachment style, as they provide an easy escape route from emotional engagement. To enhance your emotional availability, it's essential to set boundaries around these distractions.

Create 'tech-free' zones or times, such as during meals or specific 'couple times,' where devices are set aside. This practice not only minimizes interruptions but also shows your commitment to being present. Discuss these boundaries with your partner, explaining that this is a way for you to ensure you are entirely with them, unencumbered by the outside world. Such actions help in building trust and reassure your partner of your involvement and interest in the relationship.

Opening up about your feelings is perhaps one of the most challenging aspects for those with an avoidant attachment style. Yet, it's also one of the most crucial for deepening intimacy. Emotional openness involves sharing your thoughts, feelings, and vulnerabilities, which can be daunting if your natural inclination is to protect yourself from potential hurt. However, consider this openness not as a floodgate but as a gradual stream, where you share more as you feel safer and more comfortable.

Start small by expressing thoughts or feelings about neutral topics and gradually work towards more personal disclosures. Share your apprehensions about opening up with your partner; often, just acknowledging these fears can make them less daunting. This level of honesty can significantly enhance intimacy, as it invites your partner to understand and support you in your journey towards greater openness.

To practically enhance emotional presence, engage in shared mindfulness or reflection sessions with your partner. These could be as simple as spending a few minutes each day sitting together quietly, each focusing on your breath or the sensations of the moment, then sharing your experiences and feelings about the exercise. Alternatively, engage in reflection sessions where you discuss your day's highs and lows, focusing on expressing and listening to emotions without judgment or solutions. These exercises not only improve your mindfulness skills but also build a routine of emotional sharing and presence, reinforcing the emotional connection between you and your partner.

Through these practices, you can transform your approach to relationships, moving from a place of avoidance to one of engagement. By becoming more present, minimizing distractions, opening up emotionally, and practicing mindfulness with your partner, you pave the way for a deeper, more fulfilling emotional intimacy. This path, much like a walk through a blossoming garden, becomes more rewarding with every step you take together.

Active Listening: Techniques for Empathetic Engagement

Active listening is not about hearing the words spoken by another; it's a dynamic and fully engaged process where you delve into the emotional subtext of what's being shared. For individuals with a dismissive and avoidant attachment style, mastering this skill is akin to learning a new language—a language where silence speaks as loudly as words and where the spaces between sentences are filled with meaning. This approach to communication transforms interactions from mere exchanges of information to profound opportunities for connection, making it a valuable resource for anyone looking to deepen their relationships.

A primary barrier to effective active listening, especially for those who lean toward avoidant attachment, is the instinct to prepare a response while the other person is still talking. This mental rehearsal can prevent you from fully engaging with the speaker's emotions. It might even lead to misunderstandings, as you're more focused on your reply than on the speaker's actual feelings and needs. Another common hurdle is the distraction of one's own emotional reactions. If a topic touches a nerve, you might find yourself reacting internally instead of listening, which can skew the interpretation of what the other person is saying. Overcoming these barriers starts with awareness. By recognizing these tendencies, you can consciously choose to set aside your responses and reactions, creating space to truly hear not only the words but also the feelings behind them.

Techniques such as mirroring and validation can be incredibly effective in enhancing your active listening skills. Mirroring is the practice of repeating back what the speaker has said, using similar phrases, and matching their tone and pace. This technique shows that you are paying attention and also gives the speaker a chance to hear their own words reflected back to them, which can be very powerful. For example, if a partner expresses frustration about having too much on their plate, you might mirror with, "It sounds like you're feeling really overwhelmed by all your commitments right now." This not only confirms that you've understood their message but also opens the door for deeper emotional sharing.

Validation goes a step further by acknowledging the emotions behind the words. It involves recognizing and affirming the speaker's feelings as understandable and legitimate, regardless of whether you agree with the rationale behind them. Using the previous example, validating might look like adding, "It makes sense you'd feel this way given how much you have to juggle." Validation helps build emotional safety and trust, showing the speaker that their feelings are respected and valued.

For practical application, consider setting up scenarios where you can practice active listening with a partner or friend. One effective exercise is the "Emotion Exchange," where each person shares something that made them feel a strong emotion that day. The listener's job is to use both mirroring and validation to respond. This technique not only enhances your listening skills but also enhances your emotional connection with the speaker by focusing exclusively on understanding and validating their experience without shifting the focus to your own reactions or advice. These practices, when performed regularly, can significantly improve the quality of your interactions, making your relationships more fulfilling and emotionally rich.

Expressing Affection: Finding Your Love Language

Understanding how you express and receive affection can feel like discovering a map of your emotional landscape and that of your partner. This map is not universal; each person's is uniquely crafted by their experiences, preferences, and deepest needs. The concept of love languages was initially introduced by Dr. Gary Chapman. It implies that everyone has a particular way they prefer to give and receive love, which he categorizes into five distinct languages: Acts of

Service, Quality Time, Receiving Gifts, Words of Affirmation, and Physical Touch. Knowing and understanding your own primary love language, as well as that of your partner, can transform the way you connect and support each other, moving beyond misunderstandings to a place of deeper mutual satisfaction.

For someone with an avoidant attachment style, diving into the nuances of love languages might initially seem overwhelming or overly sentimental. However, embracing this exploration can provide you with valuable tools to navigate your relationships more effectively. Start by observing how you naturally express affection. Do you find yourself offering help or doing things for those you care about? Perhaps you're more inclined to give thoughtful gifts or spend quality time with loved ones. Reflect on what actions or words from others make you feel most appreciated and loved. These reflections are your first clues in discovering your love languages.

Once you have a sense of your own preferences, engage in open discussions with your partner about their love languages. This conversation can be eye-opening, revealing not just how each of you wants to be loved but also highlighting any gaps between your expressions of affection and your partner's perceptions of them. For instance, if your primary love language is Acts of Service but your partner's is Words of Affirmation, your practical help might not be perceived by them as affectionate as when you articulate your love and appreciation verbally.

Tailoring your expressions of affection to align with your partner's love language can significantly enhance the emotional intimacy in your relationship. If your partner cherishes Quality Time, consciously setting aside periods to be together undistracted can make them feel deeply valued. This might involve regular date nights but also less formal moments like walking together or sharing a hobby. If their language is Receiving Gifts, these don't have to be extravagant; often, it's the thoughtfulness and the fact that you remembered that carries the most weight. A small, meaningful gift can speak volumes about your care and attention.

Creative expressions of love are compelling because they break the routine and show that you are genuinely investing in the relationship. These can range from writing a heartfelt note or poem, creating a piece of art, cooking a special meal, or planning a surprise that you know they'll love. Such gestures make the expression of love both fun and deeply personal, adding a layer of richness to your interactions that routine expressions of affection might miss.

Incorporating regular, small acts of affection into your daily life helps maintain and deepen the connection between you and your partner, ensuring that the relationship continues to thrive. Simple actions like a morning text to wish them a good day, a touch on the arm as you walk past, or taking over a chore they dislike when they're tired can all be powerful affirmations of love. These gestures, especially when aligned with your partner's love language, reinforce your presence and commitment, making them feel continually loved and appreciated.

By engaging with the concept of love languages, you not only become more adept at expressing your affection in ways that resonate most with your partner, but you also open yourself up to receiving love in ways that deeply fulfill you. This mutual understanding and adaptation can foster a profound emotional intimacy, turning everyday interactions into opportunities for connection and affection, and transforming your relationship into a nurturing, supportive partnership.

Receiving Love: Overcoming the Discomfort of Being Cared For

Often, the act of receiving love can feel as complex and nuanced as giving it, especially for those who have woven a fabric of self-reliance so tightly around themselves that the threads seem inseparable from their very being. For someone with a dismissive and avoidant attachment style, the discomfort in accepting care and affection isn't merely a quirk; it's a deeply ingrained response shaped by past hurts and the protective barriers erected in their wake. Understanding the origins of this discomfort is the first step toward transformation. It's not uncommon for individuals like you to have experienced relationships where vulnerability was met with inconsistency or disregard. These experiences can teach you, albeit subconsciously, that reliance on others is fraught with the risk of disappointment or pain. Thus begins the cycle of self-sufficiency where you might find yourself dismissing acts of love and care, not because you don't need them, but because they stir an ancient fear of what it might cost to accept them.

Building receptiveness to love is akin to tending a garden that has long been left untended, where the soil of trust must be nurtured before it can yield connection. This cultivation often requires a conscious leaning into vulnerability, a word that might resonate with anxiety in your ears. Begin by identifying small, manageable moments where vulnerability feels less threatening. It could be as simple as accepting a compliment with a genuine 'thank you' rather than deflecting it or allowing a friend to help you with a task without brushing off the need for assistance. These moments, though seemingly insignificant, are powerful in challenging your instinct to distance and self-protect. They gradually lay down new patterns of interaction where receiving care strengthens, rather than diminishes, your sense of self.

Incorporating gratitude practices provides a practical framework for enhancing your receptiveness to love. Start a daily gratitude journal dedicated to acknowledging acts of love and kindness you experience. This might include a partner's thoughtful gesture, a friend's supportive message, or a colleague's helpful input. The act of writing them downshifts your focus from self-sufficiency to interdependence, highlighting the beauty and strength in connections. Over time, this practice not only makes you more aware of the love you are offered but also softens the internal barriers that might have made receiving love uncomfortable. It transforms acknowledgment into a habit, slowly dismantling the walls built around your capacity to be cared for.

The relationship between self-worth and the ability to receive love is particularly poignant. At its core, the struggle with accepting love often mirrors a deeper battle with feeling worthy of such affection. Enhancing self-esteem, therefore, becomes crucial in this context. Engage in activities and practices that reinforce your value not just to others but to yourself. This could be through skills development, creative expression, or wellness practices that foster a stronger sense of self and accomplishment. Additionally, therapy or counseling can provide a supportive space to explore and heal the wounds that might be tethering your self-worth to self-sufficiency. As your perception of self-worth strengthens, so does your ability to accept love without apprehension, allowing you to experience relationships in their fullest, most nourishing capacity.

Navigating the nuances of receiving love when you have an avoidant attachment style is not about altering who you are but expanding your understanding of how you relate to yourself and others. It's about gently unpacking the layers of protection to find that beneath them lies not just a need for independence but a genuine desire for connection and affection. As you continue to explore these aspects of your emotional world, remember that each step towards allowing yourself to be cared for is a step towards a more prosperous life.

The Importance of Physical Touch in Building Connection

In the landscape of human interaction, physical touch acts as a powerful, unspoken language capable of conveying a spectrum of emotions without a single word being exchanged. For someone with a dismissive and avoidant attachment style, the notion of physical touch might stir a mix of longing and discomfort, revealing a complex relationship with this form of communication. Yet, understanding and integrating touch in your interactions can significantly enhance your sense of connection, providing a tangible expression of care, comfort, and affection that words alone might not fully capture.

Touch serves as a bridge between individuals, a way to communicate empathy, love, and support directly through physical contact. It has the unique ability to soothe anxieties, calm fears, and elevate happiness, releasing oxytocin—often referred to as the 'love hormone'—which creates a sense of trust and bonding. However, the key to harnessing the positive effects of touch lies in mutual comfort and consent. This means being attuned to not only your boundaries and preferences but also those of your partner. Establishing a clear understanding and respect for each other's comfort levels with touch is crucial. This could involve discussions about what types of touch are comforting and which ones might trigger discomfort or anxiety, ensuring that physical contact remains a source of comfort and connection.

Exploring the varieties of touch can further enrich your relationship, allowing you and your partner to discover which forms of physical contact best convey affection and create closeness. Touch varies widely in its forms and implications—gentle caresses, holding hands, hugs, playful nudges, or even a reassuring pat on the back can all strengthen bonds, depending on the individual's preferences. For instance, while one person might find hand-holding during a walk a comforting gesture of connection, another might appreciate a supportive hug after a challenging day. Paying attention to how different types of touch affect you and your partner's emotions and comfort can guide you in using this empowering tool more effectively.

Introducing exercises to explore and increase physical intimacy safely can be beneficial, especially for those who find navigating physical closeness challenging. Begin with simple exercises like sitting close enough to allow your arms or knees to touch lightly when talking or watching a movie. This minimal contact can be a non-threatening way to start breaking down barriers of physical distance. Gradually, you might move on to more direct forms of touch, like exchanging massages, which not only foster physical connection but also provide relaxation and stress relief. Another exercise is the 'hand on heart' practice, where you and your partner place your hands on each other's hearts and synchronize your breathing for a few minutes. This exercise not only increases physical intimacy but also creates a profound emotional connection, as you literally feel each other's heartbeats.

By embracing physical touch as a vital component of your relationships, you can deepen your connections in a profoundly tangible way. This exploration allows you to communicate in the universal language of touch, transcending the barriers that words sometimes cannot overcome. It fosters a closeness that can be both comforting and healing, providing a solid foundation upon which trust and intimacy can flourish.

As we conclude this exploration of deepening emotional intimacy through physical touch and other means, we see how integral these elements are to cultivating fulfilling relationships. This chapter has opened doors to understanding and leveraging the power of presence, listening, affection, and touch—each acting as a vital thread in the fabric of relational connection. As we transition into the next chapter, we carry forward the understanding that our methods of communication—be it through words, actions, or touch—serve not just to convey information but to weave deeper, more meaningful bonds with those around us.

Chapter 10
Navigating Emotional Detox

Think about a dam holding back a vast lake, the pressure of the water symbolizing suppressed emotions that have built up over the years. For someone with a dismissive and avoidant attachment style, releasing this emotional pressure gradually and safely is akin to carefully opening the dam's gates—a process that can be transformative but must be approached with caution and intention. This chapter explores emotional detox, a crucial step towards healing and fostering healthier, more fulfilling relationships.

Emotional Detox: Letting Go of Suppressed Feelings

Emotional suppression involves consciously or unconsciously avoiding or inhibiting emotional expressions, a common trait you might recognize in yourself as someone with an avoidant attachment style. Over time, this can create a heavy burden, impacting not only mental health but also the quality of your relationships. The act of suppressing feelings often stems from past experiences where expressing emotions felt unsafe or was met with negative responses. This defensive mechanism, while protective at first, can lead to a buildup of unresolved emotions, manifesting as anxiety, depression, or physical symptoms like fatigue or discomfort.

Emotional detox is a process akin to cleansing the body of toxins, but instead, it focuses on purging negative emotional residues that have accumulated over time. The first step in this process is identifying the emotions you have been suppressing. This might involve recognizing patterns of behavior that mask your true feelings, such as using humor to deflect serious conversations or withdrawing when feeling hurt. Following identification, the next step is acceptance. This involves acknowledging these feelings without judgment and understanding that they are a natural response to your experiences.

Acceptance paves the way for the release of these suppressed emotions, a step that requires both courage and vulnerability. Releasing emotions might involve expressing them through words in therapy or creative activities or allowing yourself to experience and process these feelings internally. This stage is crucial for healing, as it not only helps reduce the emotional load but also decreases the need for avoidant defenses, leading to more authentic engagements in your relationships.

To facilitate the safe expression of these pent-up emotions, guided exercises can be incredibly beneficial. One effective exercise is the "Emotion Release Letter," where you write a letter to someone who has hurt you or to yourself, expressing all the feelings you've held back. You don't need to send this letter; the act of writing it is purely for your emotional release. Another exercise is the "Two-Chair Technique," used in Gestalt therapy, where you dialogue between two parts of yourself—the part that suppresses emotions and the part that wants to express them. This exercise can help you understand internal conflict and negotiate a healthier way of dealing with your feelings.

The importance of building a safe emotional space for yourself during this detox process cannot be overstressed. This involves setting boundaries with others, ensuring you have privacy and time for your detox activities, and possibly creating a physical space that feels secure and comforting. It might also involve choosing a specific time for these activities when you are least likely to be disturbed. This safe space is your sanctuary where you can explore and express your emotions without fear of judgment or interruption, facilitating a more effective and profound healing process.

In navigating this emotional detox, remember that the journey is deeply personal and can vary greatly in its duration and intensity. What matters most is your commitment to moving through this process at a pace that feels right for you, using tools and techniques that resonate with your unique emotional landscape. As you gradually open the gates to release these long-held waters, you allow for new streams of experience and emotion to flow into your life, enriching your relationships with others and, most importantly, with yourself.

Techniques for Safe Emotional Release

In the realm of emotional detox, finding effective strategies for releasing pent-up feelings is akin to discovering the right keys to unlock doors long closed. Among these keys, breathwork and movement exercises stand out as powerful tools. These practices delve into the physiological side of emotional management, helping you channel and release emotions through physical activity. Breathwork, for example, involves various breathing techniques that alter your body's response to stress and anxiety, guiding your system from a state of arousal to one of calm. This shift is crucial when emotions feel overwhelming. Simple techniques such as the 4-7-8 breathing method, where you breathe in for four seconds, hold for seven seconds, and exhale for eight seconds, can significantly calm the nervous system. This method not only helps in managing the immediate symptoms of stress but also, over time, can change how your body reacts to emotional triggers.

Moving your body can be equally transformative. Yoga, for instance, combines physical postures and controlled breathing to enhance bodily awareness and relaxation. The gentle stretches and poses open up areas where emotional tension is held, such as the shoulders and the chest, areas often constricted during times of stress. For you, engaging in regular yoga practice might not just be a way to improve physical health but also a profound method to connect with and release deep-seated emotions. Similarly, dance therapy, which involves expressive movement to improve emotional, mental, and physical integration, can be particularly liberating. Through dance, you allow your body to speak the words that your voice may not yet be able to express, moving through emotions literally and metaphorically.

Creative expression is another avenue that offers a safe passage for emotions that might seem too intense or difficult to articulate. Activities like writing, drawing, or making music provide a conduit for your feelings, transforming them into art. In writing, for instance, you can channel your emotions into characters, scenarios, or poetry, allowing you to step back and analyze these emotions from a different perspective. This not only gives you a clearer understanding of your feelings but also helps in diluting their intensity, making them more manageable. Drawing or painting can be similarly therapeutic, offering a canvas on which to color your internal emotional landscape. The strokes, the choice of colors, and the forms that emerge can all provide insights into feelings you might not have been consciously aware of. Music, whether creating or listening, can resonate with your emotions on a primal level, providing both an outlet for expression and a form of comfort.

The journey of emotional detox often requires support, and this is where the value of a trusted support network comes into play. Opening up to friends, family, or professionals about the struggles you are facing can provide not only relief but also guidance. Sharing your life experiences with someone who understands and supports you can be incredibly validating and encouraging. It is essential, however, to choose whom to confide in wisely; the goal is to feel safe and supported, not judged or misunderstood. In some cases, help from a therapist or counselor can be crucial. They can offer not only a skilled listening ear but also professional techniques and insights that can aid in deeper emotional processing.

Grounding techniques are essential tools that help you stay present and centered during this process of emotional release. Techniques such as visualization, where you picture your feet growing roots that extend deep into the earth, can help anchor your sense of self when emotions threaten to overwhelm you. Physical grounding methods, like holding onto a piece of ice, can draw your attention away from emotional distress to the immediate physical sensation, helping you manage overwhelming feelings. These practices ensure that your emotional detox does not become overwhelming, allowing you to engage with your emotions on a more manageable level.

As you explore these techniques for safe emotional release, you may find that some resonate more deeply with you than others. The key is to maintain an open mind and a willing heart, permitting yourself to explore various avenues of expression and release. Each step you take in this process, no matter how small, is a vital part of reshaping your relationship with your emotions, paving the way for a balanced emotional life.

The Role of Self-Compassion in Healing Avoidant Attachment

In the realm of personal growth, especially for someone navigating the complexities of avoidant attachment, self-compassion emerges as a gentle but powerful ally. At its core, self-compassion is treating yourself with the same kindness, concern, and support you would offer a good friend when faced with difficulties. This concept, rooted in the understanding that everyone is imperfect and life is inherently challenging, shifts your perspective from isolation to a shared human experience. For you, self-compassion is vital because it counters the harsh self-judgment that often accompanies feelings of unworthiness and fear of intimacy. By adopting a more compassionate self-view, you begin to dismantle the critical inner narratives that drive avoidant behaviors, paving the way for more nurturing relationships with both yourself and others.

Embracing self-compassion means acknowledging your emotional wounds without self-reproach. This acknowledgment is crucial, as it allows you to see your defensive detachment not as a flaw but as a response to past experiences that did not validate your emotional needs. With this understanding, you can start to reframe your relationship with yourself—one where mistakes are seen as opportunities for growth rather than reflections of inadequacy. This reframing is particularly transformative, as it encourages a mindset where seeking connection does not equate to vulnerability but to strength and self-discovery.

Integrating self-compassion into your daily life can begin with simple affirmations that reinforce compassionate self-talk. Phrases like "I am doing my best" or "It's okay to feel this way" can be powerful reminders to treat yourself with kindness. Additionally, engaging in daily mindfulness practices can enhance your self-compassion. Mindfulness encourages you to carefully watch your thoughts and feelings without judgment, fostering a non-critical awareness of your emotional state. This practice can be especially useful when dealing with moments of self-doubt or criticism, common triggers for avoidant withdrawal. By noticing these moments without immediately reacting to them, you provide space to choose a more compassionate response.

Setting aside time for activities that are fulfilling for your body and mind is another way to practice self-compassion. Whether it's reading a book, hiking, or engaging in a hobby that you enjoy, these actions offer respite from the rigors of daily life and a way to honor your needs and interests. Importantly, these moments of self-care send a message to your subconscious that you are worthy of care and attention, countering feelings of unworthiness and fostering a healthier self-image.

The inner critic can be particularly vociferous for those with avoidant attachment, often reinforcing the impulse to withdraw from emotional closeness as a way to avoid perceived shortcomings. To combat this, it's useful to first become aware of the critical inner voice. Recognize when you're being self-critical and identify the situations that trigger this criticism. Often, these are moments where you perceive a risk of rejection or judgment. Once you are aware of these patterns, challenge them by asking yourself whether you would say what you're telling yourself to a friend. If the answer is no, it's likely your inner critic speaking, not your true self.

Replacing critical thoughts with compassionate ones involves consciously choosing to speak to yourself with kindness. When you catch yourself slipping into self-criticism, pause and reframe the thought to something more supportive. For example, change "I can't believe I messed up" to "Everyone makes mistakes, I can learn from this." Over time, this practice diminishes the power of the inner critic, making way for a more supportive inner dialogue that champions your growth and well-being.

The benefits of self-compassion extend beyond personal healing; they significantly impact your relationships. As you become kinder to yourself, your capacity for emotional openness increases. This openness allows for deeper connections with others, as you are less likely to withdraw from interactions out of fear of judgment. Furthermore, self-compassion fosters resilience against relationship setbacks. By maintaining a compassionate perspective, you're better equipped to handle conflicts and misunderstandings without resorting to defensive withdrawal.

In relationships, your practice of self-compassion models healthy emotional responses and encourages mutual support and understanding. It allows you to approach interactions with less defensiveness and more genuine curiosity and care, which can transform the dynamics of your relationships. Whether it's with a partner, family, or friends, the empathy and kindness you cultivate within yourself set the tone for your interactions, making them more nurturing and connected.

By embracing and practicing self-compassion, you not only heal and improve your relationship with yourself but also create a foundation for fulfilling relationships with others. This shift is crucial for anyone working to overcome avoidant attachment, as it supports a life where closeness is not something to be feared but to be embraced with confidence and genuine affection.

Rebuilding Your Emotional Toolbox: Skills for Connection

Navigating the complexities of relationships with a dismissive and avoidant attachment style often feels like attempting to solve a puzzle without all the pieces. This missing link usually lies within the realm of emotional skills, which are crucial for building and maintaining healthy, fulfilling relationships. These skills, including emotional literacy, empathy, and effective communication, form the core of your emotional toolbox, enabling you to connect with others in more meaningful and satisfying ways.

The foundation of any strong relationship is built on several key emotional skills: self-awareness, regulation of emotions, and responsiveness to the emotions of others. Self-awareness involves understanding your feelings, triggers, and the behaviors that follow. This insight allows you to navigate personal and interpersonal challenges more effectively. Regulation of emotions, on the other hand, involves managing your reactions to feelings, especially in stressful or emotionally charged situations. This doesn't mean suppressing your feelings but rather acknowledging them and deciding how best to express them. Responsiveness to others' emotions entails recognizing and respecting the feelings of others, a skill that fosters empathy and closeness. Developing these skills enhances your ability to engage in relationships with a sense of confidence and calm, even in the face of emotional challenges.

Emotional literacy is your ability to identify, understand, and express emotions in a healthy way. It starts with broadening your emotional vocabulary, which allows for a more precise understanding of what you are feeling. For instance, recognizing whether you are feeling irritable or anxious can determine how you might address these feelings. Techniques such as emotional journaling can be a practical tool here. By regularly writing about your feelings, you can start to see the patterns in your emotional responses and triggers. This practice not only deepens your understanding of your emotional experiences but also enhances your ability to communicate these emotions to others, reducing misunderstandings and conflicts in your relationships.

Empathy is the ability to comprehend and share the feelings of others. It is particularly challenging if you tend to distance yourself emotionally. However, developing empathy is possible and immensely rewarding, as it deepens your connections and makes your interactions more fulfilling. Start by practicing active emotional listening, which involves paying full attention to the speaker and acknowledging their feelings without immediately giving advice or sharing your own experiences. This focus allows you to genuinely understand the other person's perspective. Additionally, engaging in role-reversal exercises, where you imagine yourself in someone else's situation, can enhance your empathetic reach. Over time, these practices help you develop a more instinctive, empathetic response in your interactions, making your relationships more prosperous and more reciprocal.

Effective communication is more than exchanging information; it involves actively listening, processing the information, and responding in a way that advances mutual understanding. Active listening is a skill where you need to fully concentrate, understand, respond, and then remember what is being said. In practice, this means not just listening to respond but listening to understand. Techniques such as paraphrasing what the other person has said and asking clarifying questions not only demonstrate that you are paying attention but also ensure that you have understood their point correctly. On the other hand, assertive expression involves stating your needs clearly and respectfully without passive aggression or aggression. This can be practiced through 'I' statements, such as "I feel [emotion] when [situation] because [reason]," which express your perspective without blaming or criticizing the other person. These communication skills are essential for building trust and respect in any relationship, allowing for more open and honest interactions.

By continuously working on these emotional skills, you gradually equip yourself with the necessary tools to foster healthier and more satisfying relationships. Each skill enhances your ability to interact with others in ways that respect both your needs and the needs of those around you, ultimately leading to a more connected and fulfilling life.

From Isolation to Integration: Steps Towards Emotional Openness

In navigating the landscape of emotional connections, the shift from isolation to integration may feel like stepping into sunlight after a long time in the shade. It can be both invigorating and intimidating, especially when you've grown accustomed to a solitary existence that feels safe but limiting. The tendency towards isolation isn't just a habit for someone with an avoidant attachment style—it's a protective strategy. However, the comfort it offers is often superficial and fleeting, and the longing for deeper, more meaningful connections persists, urging you to venture beyond these self-imposed boundaries.

Challenging this isolation requires a conscious decision to engage more fully with the world around you. This doesn't mean a drastic overhaul of your lifestyle but relatively small, manageable steps that encourage more frequent and meaningful interactions. Start by identifying activities or groups that align with your interests or values, as these can provide a natural and less daunting setting for social interactions. Engaging in community activities, whether a book club, a cooking class, or volunteer work, can foster a sense of belonging and shared purpose, which naturally diminishes feelings of isolation. Each small interaction in these settings is a step towards building a comfort zone with emotional openness, allowing you to gradually replace reticence with curiosity and connection.

Building and expanding your social networks is another crucial step in this process. The goal here is to cultivate a network that supports and enriches your life, understanding that the quality of connections often outweighs quantity. Start by reaching out to current acquaintances or friends with whom you've lost touch. Rekindling these relationships can be less intimidating than starting from scratch and can provide a comforting sense of familiarity. As you become more comfortable in these interactions, gradually extend your circle to include new contacts who share similar interests or experiences. Remember, the pace at which you expand this network should feel comfortable for you, respecting your need for personal space and time to recharge.

As you challenge your isolation and build your social networks, you'll inevitably face the risks associated with intimacy. These risks—vulnerability, potential rejection, and emotional exposure—are often magnified in your perception, but they are a natural part of developing closer relationships. To navigate these fears, start by setting clear personal boundaries that help you feel safe. Communicate these boundaries clearly with those around you to ensure mutual respect and understanding. Additionally, intimacy should be approached incrementally; share small bits of personal information or feelings and observe how they are received. Positive responses will reinforce your confidence in opening up more, while less supportive reactions can be valuable learning experiences, helping you refine your approach and expectations.

Celebrating small wins is essential in this transformative process. Each successful interaction, each moment of genuine connection, and every step out of your comfort zone deserves recognition and celebration. These milestones, no matter how small, signify your progress towards a more connected and emotionally rich life. They serve as reminders of your capability to change and adapt, reinforcing your resilience and encouraging continued growth.

As you integrate these new practices into your life, you'll notice a gradual shift in how you relate to others and yourself. The journey from isolation to integration is not linear or predictable, but it is filled with opportunities for personal growth and deeper human connections. Embrace each step, challenge, and victory as part of a broader transformation that enhances not only your relationships but also your overall well-being.

As we wrap up this chapter on navigating emotional detox, we've explored practical strategies to challenge isolation, build social networks, manage the risks of intimacy, and celebrate the victories along the way. These steps are not just about overcoming avoidant attachment but about enriching your life with fulfilling relationships and a robust emotional network. As we move forward, we carry with us the tools and insights needed to continue building a life marked by meaningful connections and emotional depth.

Chapter 11
Sustaining Growth and Connection

The journey of reshaping your attachment style requires persistence and adaptability. As the book comes to an end, we will explore how to maintain momentum and prevent backsliding. Identifying triggers, building a robust support system, and conducting regular self-check-ins are crucial. Embracing flexibility and adapting your methods as you and your relationships evolve ensures continued growth. Celebrating progress, no matter how insignificant reinforces positive behaviors and fuels motivation. By actively engaging with these practices, you empower yourself to build more secure and fulfilling relationships, transforming obstacles into opportunities for deeper emotional resilience and connectivity.

Maintaining Momentum: Strategies to Prevent Backsliding

As you navigate the intricacies of reshaping your attachment style, maintaining the momentum of your growth is crucial. The road to more fulfilling connections is not always a straight path; it can have its share of setbacks and challenges. Here, we explore concrete steps to keep you moving forward, even when the terrain gets tough.

Firstly, understanding what triggers your avoidant behaviors is essential. A trigger could be anything that brings up feelings of vulnerability or fear—perhaps a partner's comment that feels too intrusive or a friend asking for more commitment in the relationship. These triggers can often lead to an automatic retreat into old patterns of avoidance. To manage this, start by mapping out situations that have historically made you feel the need to pull back. Recognize these patterns and the emotions they stir within you. With this awareness, you can begin to prepare more mindful responses. For example, if you know that discussions about future plans with your partner make you anxious, you could pre-plan how to communicate your feelings and needs effectively during such conversations. This preparation not only reduces the stress associated with these triggers but also empowers you to handle them without reverting to avoidant tendencies.

Another pivotal element in sustaining your growth is building a robust support system. This network should include friends, family members, or professionals who know your goals and are committed to helping you achieve them. These individuals can offer encouragement, provide a sounding board for your concerns, and remind you of how far you've come when you find yourself faltering. If forming such connections feels daunting, consider joining support groups where you can meet others who are also working to overcome avoidant attachment. In these groups, you can share experiences, offer mutual support, and learn from each other's journeys. The empathy and understanding from these interactions can be incredibly reaffirming and can strengthen your resolve to continue on this path.

Committing to regular check-ins with yourself and your relationships can also play an important role in maintaining your growth. These check-ins serve as moments to reflect on recent interactions and assess how aligned they are with your new ways of connecting. Ask yourself questions like, "Am I communicating my needs clearly?" "How am I handling discomfort in my relationships?" and "What progress have I made in managing my triggers?". If you are in a relationship, these check-ins can also involve open discussions with your partner about how you both feel the relationship is evolving. These conversations can reinforce transparency and mutual understanding, fostering a stronger bond and a supportive environment for continual growth.

Lastly, the strategies you employ to manage your avoidant attachment need to evolve as you and your relationships do. The techniques that helped you at the beginning of your growth journey might not be as effective as your situations and relationships develop. Stay flexible in adjusting your methods. For instance, if you find that journaling no longer provides the insight it once did, you might switch to more interactive forms of reflection like therapy or mentorship. Similarly, as your relationships deepen, the ways you communicate and maintain boundaries may need to be recalibrated to accommodate deeper levels of intimacy and understanding.

By actively engaging with these strategies—identifying triggers, creating a support system, conducting regular check-ins, and adapting your methods—you equip yourself to continue making progress. Each step taken and each strategy implemented fortifies your path toward more secure and fulfilling relationships, ensuring that backsliding becomes less of an obstacle and more of a stepping stone toward deeper emotional resilience and connectivity.

Celebrating Progress: Recognizing and Rewarding Change

Acknowledging your growth in emotional and relational areas is pivotal, especially when you've historically leaned towards dismissive and avoidant attachment styles. Recognizing the strides you've made, no matter how minor they might seem, serves as a testament to your resilience and commitment to evolving beyond old patterns. This recognition isn't merely about self-congratulation; it's an essential practice that fuels your ongoing motivation and reinforces the positive changes that you're integrating into your daily life.

Think of your progress like milestones on a map marking the significant turns you've taken on your path towards more meaningful connections. Each milestone represents a moment of overcoming, a point where you chose a different reaction than what your instincts might have dictated. Maybe it was a time you maintained a conversation even though you felt like withdrawing, or perhaps it was a moment when you expressed your needs clearly in a relationship despite fears of vulnerability. Acknowledging these moments involves more than a mere mental note; it requires a conscious reflection that solidifies the importance of these changes. Creating a ritual around this acknowledgment can be particularly impactful. For instance, you might keep a 'victory log'—a dedicated journal where you record your personal growth. Regularly updating this log not only provides you with a tangible record of your progress but also boosts your emotional morale on tougher days.

Celebrating these milestones is equally important. Celebrations imprint on our emotional memories, reinforcing the behaviors that led to our achievements. These need not be grand gestures; small, personal celebrations can be profoundly meaningful. You might treat yourself to a favorite meal, a day out in nature, or a new book each time you add a significant entry to your victory log. Alternatively, for larger milestones, such as sustaining a relationship for longer than you previously managed, consider more substantial rewards like a weekend getaway. These celebrations act as incentives and reminders of the joys that your efforts toward emotional growth can yield.

Incorporating regular reflection practices enhances this process of acknowledgment and celebration. Set aside a regular time, perhaps at the end of each month, to review your victory log. During these sessions, reflect not just on what you achieved but also on how these achievements made you feel. Did opening up in a relationship bring you closer to someone? How did it feel to maintain boundaries effectively? Reflecting on these questions deepens your understanding of the value of your growth, embedding the desire to continue this positive trajectory.

Positive reinforcement, a principle rooted in behavioral psychology, plays a crucial role here. It's based on the idea that behaviors followed by favorable outcomes are far more likely to be repeated. In the context of your personal development, this means actively reinforcing your progress. Each time you recognize and celebrate your growth, you're essentially programming your mind to view these changes as rewarding, thus increasing the likelihood of you continuing to engage in these behaviors. Sharing your development with a trusted friend or mentor can also serve as a form of positive reinforcement. Their acknowledgment and praise can amplify your sense of achievement and spur you on to maintain your efforts.

By integrating these practices—acknowledging growth, celebrating milestones, engaging in regular reflection, and leveraging positive reinforcement—you create a supportive environment for sustained personal development. This environment not only fosters your growth but also transforms the process into a rewarding experience, making the path toward deeper connections a vibrant part of your life.

Community and Support Systems: Finding Your Tribe

The fabric of your life, much like a rich tapestry, is woven from threads of relationships and interactions that provide color, strength, and texture. Among these, a supportive community plays a pivotal role, not just in fostering growth in your relationships but also in enhancing your overall well-being. Think about a safety net that catches you when you fall or a cheerleading squad that celebrates your victories, no matter how small. This is what a supportive community can offer. It extends beyond mere friendship to encompass a network of relationships built on mutual respect, empathy, and shared values. For someone who tends to retreat into solitude under stress, recognizing the value of this community can be transformative, offering not just companionship but a crucial buffer against the isolation that often accompanies avoidant attachment.

Creating this support network involves more than just increasing the number of people you know; it's about cultivating meaningful connections. Start by assessing the relationships you currently have. Which of these provide a sense of comfort and encouragement? Which ones challenge you in positive ways? Strengthen these connections by investing your time and energy, engaging more deeply, and being present during your interactions. It's also beneficial to extend your network by connecting with others who share similar interests. This might feel daunting, but you can begin in familiar environments, perhaps by joining clubs, groups, or classes that align with your hobbies or passions. Engaging with other people who share your passions can provide a natural and less pressured way to form new connections.

The process of building this network should be intentional. Choose to connect with individuals who respect your need for space but also encourage you to stretch your comfort zones in healthy ways. It's important to communicate openly about your tendencies towards avoidance and how you are working to overcome these patterns. Often, you'll find that others are more understanding and supportive when they are aware of your struggles and goals. This transparency can foster deeper connections and a more supportive network.

Participation in group activities can enhance your sense of belonging and community. These activities could range from collaborative projects at work, volunteer groups, and sports teams to book clubs or art classes. The key here is engagement in shared endeavors that resonate with your personal interests and values. Such involvement not only brings the joy of collaboration but also reinforces your sense of identity and belonging within a community. Group activities provide opportunities to practice new relationship skills in a safe environment, where the focus is on the activity rather than on individual interactions. This can be particularly comforting if direct social interactions feel daunting.

Furthermore, these activities often put you in a position where mutual support is not just helpful, but necessary. This dynamic can shift your perspective on giving and receiving help, making it a more natural part of relationships. Over time, your participation can evolve into a leadership or mentoring role, providing a sense of purpose and contribution that strengthens your ties to the community.

The strength of a support system lies in its reciprocity. A healthy community thrives on give-and-take relationships where all members feel valued and supported. As you benefit from the support of others, look for opportunities to give back. This could mean offering your skills, time, or resources to those within your community who might benefit from them. Perhaps you could organize community events, offer to help someone with a project, or simply be there to listen when someone needs an ear.

Giving back strengthens the community and reinforces one's sense of self-worth and belonging. It can shift one's focus from what one needs to what one can offer, an empowering change that can alter one's perception of oneself and one's relationships. This reciprocal nature of support systems ensures that they are sustainable, as each member contributes and benefits from the collective strength of the group.

By actively engaging in these steps—building a support network, participating in group activities, and embracing the reciprocity of support systems—you create a dynamic community around you. This community does not just support your journey towards more secure and fulfilling relationships but becomes an integral part of your life's fabric, offering strength, color, and texture to your world.

The Lifelong Journey: Embracing Growth Beyond Avoidance

As you navigate the landscapes of your personal evolution, remember that this process is not a finite one. Growth, particularly when it pertains to emotional and relational development, is an ongoing endeavor. It's about continually adapting to new insights, experiences, and even setbacks, each offering unique opportunities for deeper learning and self-discovery. Unlike a book that concludes with the final page, your growth narrative is continuously being written. Each chapter builds upon the last, and with each, you are equipped to explore further into the realms of what it means to connect deeply with yourself and others.

Adapting to change is a significant theme in this ongoing story. Life is inherently dynamic—relationships evolve, personal circumstances shift, and emotional landscapes change. Embracing these new changes as opportunities rather than obstacles can transform your approach to life's inevitable fluctuations. This mindset encourages you to view each change, no matter how challenging, as a stepping stone to further growth. For instance, a shift in a close relationship might initially trigger your avoidant tendencies, prompting a retreat into solitude. However, viewing this change as a chance to explore new depths in the relationship can lead to a richer, more robust connection than before. It's about using the tools and insights you've gained to navigate these waters with a sense of curiosity and openness, allowing yourself to learn from each experience and to refine your approach continuously.

The concept of legacy might often be associated with tangible achievements or material inheritances, but there's a more profound legacy you're crafting through your relational interactions—the legacy of connection. This legacy is about the quality of relationships you nurture, the emotional bonds you strengthen, and the impact you have on those around you. It's about how you make others feel, the support you offer, and the empathy you extend. As you continue on this path, consider the relational legacy you wish to leave behind. How do you want to be remembered by friends, family, and partners? What values do you want your interactions to reflect? Answering these questions can provide a profound sense of purpose and direction in your ongoing development, guiding your decisions and actions in ways that align with your desired legacy of deep, meaningful connections.

Holistic well-being is the thread that weaves together emotional intimacy, relational health, and overall life satisfaction. It underscores the interconnectedness of various aspects of your life. Your emotional health impacts your relationships; your relationships influence your mental health, and together, they affect your overall quality of life. Approaching your growth with a holistic perspective means considering how changes in one area might enhance or detract from another. For example, improving your ability to set boundaries can lead to better emotional health, which in turn can strengthen your relationships. Similarly, nurturing supportive relationships can provide a buffer against life's stresses, contributing to better mental and physical health. By viewing your growth as a holistic process, you ensure that each step you take not only serves your immediate goals but also contributes to a broader, more balanced well-being.

As this chapter of your growth narrative draws to a close, reflect on the continuous nature of your development. Each day presents new opportunities to learn, to adapt, and to connect. The tools and insights you've gathered are not just for overcoming avoidant attachment—they are for enriching your entire life experience. Embrace each moment of this ongoing process, knowing that with each step, you are weaving a richer, more colorful tapestry of connections that will define the legacy of your relationships and your holistic well-being.

As we transition from exploring sustained growth and connection, we carry forward the understanding that personal evolution is a perpetual process, enriched by each experience and adapted through every challenge. Let this knowledge empower you as you step into a new a new journey of emotional and relational fulfillment.

Outro

As we conclude this transformative journey together, I hope you have found clarity, insights, and tools that resonate with your experiences and aspirations. From unraveling the complexities of your avoidant attachment style to embracing the possibilities of vulnerability and connection, this book has been a roadmap through the landscapes of self-awareness, emotional intimacy, and lasting change.

We embarked on this journey by laying the foundation with an understanding of avoidant attachment—how it forms and how it manifests in your relationships. Recognizing and understanding your own patterns was our first milestone and remains the bedrock of your ongoing transformation. Self-awareness is not just about identifying your tendencies to withdraw or detach; it's about gently confronting these behaviors with curiosity and compassion.

Embracing vulnerability might have felt counterintuitive initially, especially when your instinct has often been to protect yourself from potential emotional discomfort. Yet, as we explored together, vulnerability is not a sign of weakness, it is a brave first step towards building trust and intimacy. It is through letting your guard down that you allow others to truly connect with you and you with them.

Throughout these chapters, we've explored a variety of practical strategies designed to help you move away from avoidant behaviors and towards healthier, more connected relationships. From journaling to mindfulness, setting effective boundaries to enhancing your communication skills, these tools are your allies. They are meant to support you as you rewrite the narratives of your relationships and engage more authentically with those around you.

Change, especially in the realm of deep-seated attachment styles, is neither quick nor linear. It will require patience, persistence, and a lot of self-compassion. Remember, every small step you take towards opening up and every moment you choose to stay present in a relationship is a victory worth celebrating. Keep practicing, keep reflecting, and allow yourself the space and grace to grow at your own pace.

I urge you to view this book not just as a read but as a companion in your ongoing journey toward emotional freedom and more prosperous relationships. Apply the insights and strategies we've discussed diligently, and watch as your relationships begin to transform. Prioritize your emotional well-being and your relationships; they are the cornerstones of a fulfilling life.

As you continue to evolve and adapt, don't forget that your journey could be a beacon of hope for others. Sharing your experiences and progress can uplift others who might be grappling with similar challenges, creating ripples of positive change.

In closing, hold onto the hope and confidence that change is indeed possible. You have the tools, you have the knowledge, and most importantly, you have the strength to shift away from avoidant attachment towards a life rich in meaningful connections. Trust in the process, engage with your heart and believe in your capacity to transform. Your relationships—past, present, and future—are a canvas awaiting your renewed touch.

May you walk forward with confidence and courage, empowered by the knowledge that you are capable of nurturing the deep, satisfying connections you deserve? Here's to your journey—a journey of breaking free, connecting deeply, and living fully. Thank you for allowing me to be a part of your path to transformation.

References

Fraley, R. C. (n.d.). **Attachment theory and research**. Retrieved from http://labs.psychology.illinois.edu/~rcfraley/attachment.htm

Taylor, S. E., & Stanton, A. L. (2013). **Coping resources, coping processes, and mental health**. *Annual Review of Clinical Psychology, 9*(1), 377-401. Retrieved from https://www.ncbi.nlm.nih.gov/pmc/articles/PMC3774302/

Schwartz, A. (n.d.). **How relationships change the brain and heal attachment**. Retrieved from https://drarielleschwartz.com/how-relationships-change-brain-heal-attachment-dr-arielle-schwartz/

Attachment Project. (n.d.). **Avoidant attachment style**. Retrieved from https://www.attachmentproject.com/blog/avoidant-attachment-style/

Psych Central. (n.d.). **How childhood trauma affects adult relationships**. Retrieved from https://psychcentral.com/blog/how-childhood-trauma-affects-adult-relationships

Simply Psychology. (n.d.). **Dismissive-avoidant attachment style: Signs and how to heal**. Retrieved from https://www.simplypsychology.org/dismissive-avoidant-attachment-style-signs-how-to-heal.html

Teach Trauma. (n.d.). **Trauma's impact on attachment**. Retrieved from https://teachtrauma.com/information-about-trauma/traumas-impact-on-attachment/

Cleveland Clinic. (2022). **Attachment theory and attachment styles**. Retrieved from https://health.clevelandclinic.org/attachment-theory-and-attachment-styles

Attachment Project. (n.d.). **How to communicate with an avoidant partner**. Retrieved from https://www.attachmentproject.com/blog/communicate-with-avoidant-partner/

Psychology Today. (2021). **How someone's attachment style affects their social media use**. Retrieved from https://www.psychologytoday.com/ca/blog/close-encounters/202102/how-someones-attachment-style-affects-their-social-media-use

Verywell Mind. (2021). **Emotional numbing: Symptoms and causes**. Retrieved from https://www.verywellmind.com/emotional-numbing-symptoms-2797372

Psychology Help. (n.d.). **Top 7 avoidant attachment deactivating strategies**. Retrieved from https://www.psychologyhelp.com/top-7-avoidant-attachment-deactivating-strategies-best-online-avoidant-attachment-therapy/

Verywell Mind. (2022). **Fear of intimacy: Symptoms and causes**. Retrieved from https://www.verywellmind.com/fear-of-intimacy-2671818

Attachment Project. (n.d.). **Avoidant attachment relationships**. Retrieved from https://www.attachmentproject.com/avoidant-attachment-relationships/

Psych Central. (n.d.). **Ways to increase intimacy and communication with an avoidant partner**. Retrieved from https://psychcentral.com/relationships/ways-to-increase-intimacy-and-communication-with-an-avoidant-partner

Good Therapy. (2017). **Ending the anxious-avoidant dance**. Retrieved from https://www.goodtherapy.org/blog/ending-anxious-avoidant-dance-part-2-built-in-path-to-healing-0518175/

University of Reading. (2023). **How solitude boosts wellbeing**. Retrieved from [https://www.reading.ac.uk/news/2023/Research-News/

How-solitude-boosts-wellbeing](https://www.reading.ac.uk/news/2023/Research-News/How-solitude-boosts-wellbeing)

Medium. (2023). **Balancing independence and togetherness in relationships**. Retrieved from https://medium.com/@soul-facts/balancing-independence-and-togetherness-in-relationships-d3c3c00ad6ef

Taylor, S. E., & Stanton, A. L. (2023). **Coping resources, coping processes, and mental health**. *Annual Review of Clinical Psychology, 9* (1), 377-401. Retrieved from https://www.ncbi.nlm.nih.gov/pmc/articles/PMC8935176/

Insight Timer. (n.d.). **Meditation for dismissive/avoidant attachment**. Retrieved from https://insighttimer.com/attachmentrepair/guided-meditations/meditation-for-dismissive-slash-avoidant-attachment

Healthline. (2022). **Emotional triggers**. Retrieved from https://www.healthline.com/health/mental-health/emotional-triggers

PurpleSec. (2022). **Vulnerability visibility**. Retrieved from https://purplesec.us/learn/vulnerability-visibility/

Psych Central. (2022). **Somatic therapy exercises for trauma**. Retrieved from https://psychcentral.com/lib/somatic-therapy-exercises-for-trauma

Mindful. (2022). **Why self-compassion is essential to healing**. Retrieved from [https://www.mindful.org/why-self-compassion-is-essential-to-heal

ing/](https://www.mindful.org/why-self-compassion-is-essential-to-healing/)

Self Heal Journey. (2023). **Journal prompts for healing**. Retrieved from https://selfhealjourney.com/2023/06/17/journal-prompts-for-healing-2/

Stanton, A. L., & Taylor, S. E. (2016). **Coping resources, coping processes, and mental health**. *Annual Review of Clinical Psychology, 9*(1), 377-401. Retrieved from https://www.ncbi.nlm.nih.gov/pmc/articles/PMC4814782/

Attachment Project. (n.d.). **Schema therapy**. Retrieved from https://www.attachmentproject.com/blog/schema-therapy/#:~:text=Compared%20to%20CBT%2C%20Schema%20Therapy,in%20early%20childhood%20and%20adolescence

Psychology Tools. (n.d.). **Behavioral experiment**. Retrieved from https://www.psychologytools.com/resource/behavioral-experiment/

Crisis & Trauma Resource Institute. (2022). **The 5 parts of a meaningful apology**. Retrieved from [https://ctrinstitute.com/blog/the-5-parts-of-a-meaningful-apology/](https://ctrinstitute.com/blog/the-

www.ingramcontent.com/pod-product-compliance
Lightning Source LLC
Chambersburg PA
CBHW030439010526
44118CB00011B/710